THE GLUTEN-FREE KITCHEN

★ *Fresh, Easy & Feel-Good* ★

150
GREAT RECIPES

★

CONTENTS

INTRODUCTION

Gluten-free diets are on the up and up. For those with coeliac disease, it's non-negotiable. For others, eating gluten-free just makes them feel better. And for some, gluten-free is preferred for health and fitness reasons. Gluten is the protein found in many starchy carbohydrates, so omitting it tends to result in a diet higher in protein and lower in carbs, and this can mean weight loss. The jury is still out on the medical benefits of a gluten-free diet, but what is known is that naturally gluten-free foods make for healthy choices in terms of fuel for your body.

So what is naturally gluten-free? All fresh meat and poultry – tick. All dairy, eggs and fats – tick. Rice, quinoa and other gluten-free grains and flours – tick. All fresh, frozen, dried, canned and juiced fruits and vegetables – tick. All pulses, nuts and seeds – tick. That's a huge range of fresh and nutritious produce to choose from, which forms the basis of the recipes in this book.

It's also important to know what's out if you want to follow a gluten-free diet. The answer is wheat, rye, spelt and barley, often used to make bread, cakes and pasta. If you are going gluten-free, it's useful to get up close and personal with the ingredients list on any foods you buy. You might be surprised where gluten pops up – it's commonly used in soy sauce, most cereals and in anything that's crumbed or battered. And, if you fancy a cold beer on a hot day, well, you might want to consider switching to cider!

This book kicks off with an extensive Breakfast section. It's the most important meal of the day and can be a hard one to fulfil without gluten. In this section, you'll find lots of filling alternatives to cereal, such as homemade granola, chia smoothie bowls or a nourishing quinoa-based porridge.

In the Light Meals section of this book, discover a wide range of delicious soups, salads and staples that are quick and easy to whip up for lunch or a light dinner. If you are looking for a gluten-free take on that everyday

Note to the reader: Certain ingredients in this book – mainly sauces, stocks or seasonings – have been listed as 'GF' (short for gluten-free) meaning you should seek out a gluten-free variety or check the ingredients listed on the product carefully and, if in doubt, contact the manufacturer because brands differ in their inclusion of gluten in these foods.

favourite, pizza, try one of three options for wheat-free bases. Fancy a burger? Ditch the bread bun for a mighty mushroom instead.

If you fancy something more substantial or crave alternatives to familiar foods at dinner time, we've got you covered in the Main Meals section. Love lasagne? How about moussaka or shepherd's pie instead. Hanging out for a bowl of pasta? No problem, we have recipes here for zucchini-based zoodles, or even a cabbage ragu – healthy and tasty alternatives to the gluten varieties. Sunday roast at your place? You can do it the gluten-free way with the recipes in this book for a perfect roast chook and, more importantly, the stuffing and gravy to go with it, which are often secret sources of gluten.

If you are worried that gluten-free means no delicious breads or cakes, think again. In the Breads section of this book, you'll find amazing recipes for wholesome seed loaves, fluffy potato-based bread, crunchy crispbread, zucchini bread and pumpkin scones, plus a buckwheat loaf that's set to become a staple. And there are yummy cakes and desserts-a-plenty to be found here too. You don't need to miss out on doughnuts, chocolate cake, tiramisu or creme brulee: the recipes in this book will equip you with alternatives that are every bit as delicious and might even be more nutritious.

In the final section of this book, we provide some great ideas for gluten-free food and treats for the kids. It needn't be hard to make the switch. They'll won't bat an eye when you offer them sweet snickerdoodle cookies, cinnamon scrolls (made out of pumpkin, but that's just between us), raspberry brownies or black bean chocolate cake. For kids' parties, you'll find fun ideas like banana chips, Halloween cupcakes and, a certain winner, inari sushi teddies! Gluten-free can be fun, easy and a feel-good alternative for everybody in the family, so let's get cooking.

BREAKFAST

BUTTERMILK PANCAKES WITH FRESH BERRIES

INGREDIENTS

1¾ cups (175g, 6oz) coconut flour

1½ tsps GF baking powder

1 tsp GF bicarbonate of soda

½ tsp salt

2 tbsps coconut sugar

2 large eggs, room temperature, lightly beaten

2½ cups (620ml, 20fl oz) buttermilk

½ tsp vanilla extract

2 tbsps coconut oil

1 cup (125g, 4oz) fresh fruit for serving (strawberries, blueberries, raspberries, etc)

Pure maple syrup, to serve

METHOD

1. Add the flour, baking powder, bicarb, salt and sugar together in a large mixing bowl. Give them a good stir and make a well in the centre.

2. In a separate mixing bowl, whisk together the eggs, milk and vanilla.

3. Pour the wet ingredients into the dry and whisk until incorporated and you have a smooth batter.

4. Cover and let the bowl sit in the refrigerator for 30 minutes.

5. Heat a medium-sized frying pan over medium-high heat and melt a small amount of coconut oil. Pour a ¼ cup of pancake batter into the pan. Cook until bubbles appear across the surface of the pancake.

6. Flip it over and cook for 2 minutes on the other side until both sides are golden brown.

7. Place on a warm plate in a warm oven and repeat with the rest of the batter.

8. Serve the pancakes warm topped with fresh fruit of your choice and drizzled with pure maple syrup.

SERVES 4 ★ PREP 10MIN ★ COOK TIME 20MIN

QUINOA PORRIDGE WITH FRESH FRUIT

INGREDIENTS

1 cup (125g, 4oz) pecans

1 cup (170g, 6oz) raw mixed quinoa

3 cups (750ml, 24fl oz) water

¾ cup (185ml, 6fl oz) coconut milk

3 tbsps agave syrup

2 large ripe bananas, sliced

1 large red apple, cored and thinly sliced

¾ cup (75g, 3oz) fresh blueberries

Mint sprigs, to serve

METHOD

1. To toast the pecans, preheat a small frying pan over medium-high heat. Dry fry the pecans for about 4 minutes or until they start to brown. Remove the pecans immediately from the pan and set aside.
2. Rinse the quinoa in running water, then place it in a medium saucepan with the 3 cups water over medium-high heat. Bring to the boil, then reduce the heat to low and simmer, covered, for 15 minutes or until the quinoa is softened, but still has a tiny bit of crunch.
3. Pour in the coconut milk and agave, stir and heat for about 3 minutes to heat it through. Add more agave if needed.
4. Divide the quinoa between four serving bowls, along with the liquid.
5. Top with sliced banana, toasted pecans, apple slices and fresh blueberries.
6. Garnish with a sprig of mint and serve.

CREPES AND HONEY

INGREDIENTS

¾ cup (60g, 2oz)
GF oat flour

¼ tsp salt

2 large eggs, room
temperature

½ cup (125ml, 4fl oz)
milk (can use nut milk)

2 tbsps unsalted butter,
melted

Butter, for cooking

½ cup (180g, 6oz)
honey

METHOD

1. Place the flour, salt, eggs, milk and melted butter in a large mixing
   bowl and whisk together until you have a smooth batter.

2. Cover and place in the refrigerator for at least 30 minutes.

3. Heat a medium-sized frying pan over medium-high heat and melt a
   small amount of butter. Pour a ¼ cup crepe batter into the pan.

4. Cook for roughly 40 seconds, then gently flip it and cook for about
   20 seconds until both sides of the crepe are golden brown.

5. Place on a warm plate in a warm oven, cover with a towel and
   repeat with the rest of the batter until finished.

6. Serve the crepes warm, drizzled with honey.

MAKES 16 ★ PREP 30min ★ COOK TIME 1hr 10min

PUMPKIN HONEY PANCAKES

INGREDIENTS

1¾ cups (210g, 8oz) buckwheat flour

1½ tsps GF baking powder

¼ tsp GF bicarbonate of soda

⅓ cup (50g, 2oz) light brown sugar

½ tsp salt

1 cup (250ml, 8fl oz) Greek yoghurt

1 cup (250ml, 8fl oz) milk

2 tsps pure maple syrup

2 large eggs, room temperature

1 tsp vanilla extract

60g (2oz) unsalted butter, melted

½ cup (180g, 6oz) honey

¼ cup (30g, 1oz) toasted pepitas (pumpkin seeds)

Pumpkin puree

2 cups (270g, 9oz) butternut pumpkin, peeled and cut into 3cm (1in) chunks

1 tsp cinnamon

1½ tsp allspice

¼ tsp nutmeg

¼ tsp ground cloves

METHOD

1. To make the pumpkin puree, preheat oven to 160°C (325°F, Gas Mark 3) and line a large flat baking tray with baking paper. Scatter the pumpkin over the tray in an even layer and bake for 40 minutes or until mushy. Puree pumpkin in a blender until smooth with the cinnamon, allspice, nutmeg and cloves. You need ⅔ cup of puree for this recipe.

2. Mix together the flour, baking powder, bicarb, sugar and salt in a large mixing bowl.

3. In a separate mixing bowl, whisk together yoghurt, milk, pumpkin puree, syrup, eggs, vanilla and half the butter then pour into the dry ingredients and whisk to form a smooth batter.

4. Heat a medium-sized frying pan over medium-high heat and add a small amount of the remaining butter. Pour ¼ cup pancake batter into the pan. Cook until bubbles appear across the surface of the pancake. Flip it over and cook for 2 minutes on the other side until both sides are golden brown. Place on a plate in a warm oven and repeat with the rest of the batter.

5. Serve warm, drizzled with honey and pepitas.

SAVOURY OATMEAL AND BACON, EGGS AND SPROUTS

INGREDIENTS

1 cup (90g, 3oz) GF rolled oats

1 cup (250ml, 8fl oz) milk (can use nut milk)

1 cup (250ml, 8fl oz) water

1 tbsp unsalted butter

1 tsp GF onion powder

½ tsp salt

¼ tsp ground chilli

2 tbsps white vinegar

2 fresh eggs, room temperature (if they're not fresh, they won't poach)

6 rashers bacon

½ cup (50g, 2oz) loosely packed alfalfa sprouts

METHOD

1. Place the oats, milk and water in a medium saucepan over medium-high heat. Bring to a boil, then reduce the heat to low and simmer, stirring frequently for 10 minutes until the oats are soft and creamy.

2. While the oatmeal is cooking, stir in the butter, onion powder, salt and chilli.

3. Once the oatmeal is cooked through, remove it from the heat and set aside to cool for 10 minutes then divide it between two serving bowls.

4. Fry the rashers of bacon to your preferred crispiness and sit on the oatmeal.

5. To poach the eggs, heat a medium pot filled with 5cm (2in) of water and the white vinegar until barely simmering – don't let it get beyond a simmer at any time.

6. Crack an egg into a small shallow saucer. Whisk the water to create a gentle whirlpool then gently slide the egg off the saucer into the middle of the whirlpool.

7. Cook for 3 minutes until set around the outside. Gently lift out of the saucepan with a slotted spoon, drain on some paper towels then place on one of the bowls. Repeat with the second egg.

8. Top each bowl with the alfalfa sprouts and a pinch of chilli.

CHOCOLATE PORRIDGE

INGREDIENTS

½ cup (60g, 2oz) walnuts

2 tbsps chia seeds

½ cup (90g, 3oz) dried red lentils

2 cups (500ml, 1pt) water

¼ cup (60ml, 2fl oz) coconut milk

1 tbsp coconut oil

2 tbsps raw cacao powder

2 tbsps pure maple syrup

½ cup (50g, 2oz) fresh blueberries

1 small apple, cored and sliced

METHOD

1. To toast the walnuts, preheat a small frying pan over medium-high heat. Dry fry the walnuts for about 4 minutes or until they start to brown. Remove the walnuts immediately from the pan and set aside.

2. Place the chia seeds in a blender or use a stick blender to grind them to a powder

3. Place the lentils and water in a medium saucepan over medium-high heat until almost simmering. Reduce to low and simmer the lentils for 10 minutes or until mushy. Remove from heat and stir through the coconut milk and ground chia seeds. Let it sit for 30 minutes.

4. Gently reheat for 5 minutes over medium heat then add the coconut oil until melted and combined. Remove from heat.

5. Stir in the cacao powder and maple syrup to taste.

6. Divide the porridge between serving bowls and top with the toasted walnuts, blueberries and apple slices.

BLACKBERRY RICE PORRIDGE

INGREDIENTS

1 cup (155g, 4oz)
white short-grain rice

2¼ cups (560ml, 19 fl oz)
water

½ cup (125ml, 4fl oz)
coconut milk

Pinch of salt

4 tbsps agave syrup

½ tsp fresh lime juice

2 cups (200g, 8oz)
fresh blackberries

METHOD

1. Place the rice and water in a medium saucepan over medium heat. Bring to the boil, then reduce heat to low and simmer, covered for 13 minutes.

2. Check the consistency, the rice should be cooked, if not cook for another minute or so.

3. Stir in the coconut milk for 2 minutes, then remove the saucepan from the heat and let sit for 5 minutes.

4. Stir through the salt, agave and lime juice. Adjust sweetness with more agave if needed.

5. Dive between four serving bowls and serve with fresh blackberries on the side.

COTTAGE CHEESE PANCAKES

INGREDIENTS

¼ cup (25g, 1oz) coconut flour

2 tbsps almond meal

¼ tsp baking powder

Pinch of salt

2 tsps caster sugar

1 cup (225g, 8oz) cottage cheese

3 tbsps milk

2 small eggs, room temperature, separated

1 tbsp unsalted butter, melted

Butter, for frying

2 tbsps pure icing sugar

2 cups (320g, 11oz) stewed fruit of your choice

METHOD

1. Add the flour, almond meal, baking powder, salt and sugar together in a large mixing bowl. Give them a good stir and make a well in the centre.

2. In a separate mixing bowl, stir together the cottage cheese and the milk.

3. Whisk the egg yolks until they're thick and pale, then mix in the melted butter (make sure it's nearly room temperature before adding to eggs so you don't accidentally cook them).

4. Mix the eggs into the cottage cheese mixture and combine thoroughly.

5. Add the wet ingredients to the dry and combine.

6. Whisk the egg whites until stiff peaks form. Gently fold the egg whites through the cottage cheese mixture.

7. Heat a medium-sized frying pan over medium-high heat and melt a small amount of butter. Place about ⅓ cup pancake batter into the pan for each pancake. Cook until golden brown underneath for about 4 minutes and bubbles appear on the surface.

8. Gently flip over and cook for 2 minutes on the other side until both sides are golden brown.

9. Place on a warm plate in a warm oven and repeat with the rest of the batter.

10. Serve the pancakes warm onto a plate of warm stewed fruit, dusted with icing sugar.

SPINACH OMELETTE ROLLS

INGREDIENTS

6 large eggs, room temperature

1 cup (220ml, 7fl oz) milk (can use nut milk)

5 tsps arrowroot flour

Salt and pepper

1 cup (125g, 4oz) tasty cheese, grated

3 cups (90g, 3oz) packed fresh spinach, finely chopped

¼ cup (10g, ¼ oz) fresh parsley, finely chopped

Parsley leaves, to garnish

METHOD

1. Preheat the oven to 180°C (350°F, Gas Mark 4) and line a large 36 x 25cm (10in) (14 x 10in) baking tray with greased baking paper.

2. Add the eggs, milk and arrowroot to a large mixing bowl along with a couple of good grinds of salt and pepper and whisk until thoroughly combined. Pour the mixture into the baking tray.

3. Bake in the oven for 12 minutes, then remove and quickly sprinkle the cheese over the top. Return the tray to the oven and bake for 5 more minutes. Remove the omelette from the oven and let stand for 5 minutes.

4. Toss together the spinach and parsley then spread in an even layer over the omelette.

5. Gently and carefully roll up the omelette, peeling off the paper as you roll.

6. Cut the roll into 3cm (1in) slices and serve garnished with extra parsley.

CORN FRITTERS

INGREDIENTS

1½ cups (375ml, 13fl oz) milk

1 cup (160g, 6oz) fine polenta

3 tbsps unsalted butter, room temperature

1 tsp GF baking powder

Salt and pepper

1 tsp ground chilli

2 large eggs, lightly beaten, room temperature

¼ cup (25g, 1oz) spring onions, finely chopped

1 tbsp jalapenos, finely minced

1½ cups (260g, 9oz) cooked corn kernels

¼ cup (25g, 1oz) chickpea flour

2 tbsps olive oil, for frying

METHOD

1. Stir half the milk and the polenta in a mixing bowl. Set aside.

2. Heat the rest of the milk in a saucepan over medium heat until almost simmering. Turn the heat down and slowly whisk in the polenta mixture and the butter then stir for 10 minutes until thickened.

3. Remove the saucepan from the heat and pour the mixture back into a large mixing bowl. Whisk through all the other ingredients except the olive oil until almost combined.

4. Heat a large frying pan over medium-high heat and heat half the olive oil. Spoon out ¼ cup-sized amounts of fritter batter into the pan. Fry for 5 minutes on one side until golden brown then flip over and cook for about 2 minutes until cooked through and golden brown on both sides.

5. Place the cooked fritters a warm plate in a warm oven, covered with a tea towel, and repeat with the rest of the batter.

6. Serve the fritters warm.

EGGS ROYALE WITH HOMEMADE HOLLANDAISE

INGREDIENTS

4 fresh medium eggs, room temperature (if they're not fresh, they won't poach)

2 tbsps white vinegar

4 slices GF bread

8 slices smoked salmon

Olive oil, to garnish

2 tbsps micro greens, to garnish

Hollandaise sauce

3 medium egg yolks, room temperature

1 tbsp lemon juice

125g (4oz) unsalted butter, cubed, room temperature

Pinch of cayenne pepper

Salt and pepper

METHOD

1. To make the sauce, whisk the egg yolks with the lemon juice in a heatproof bowl until light and frothing.

2. Place the bowl over a pot of simmering water and keep whisking until mixture starts to thicken.

3. Add a couple of cubes of butter at a time, whisking until they're melted and incorporated. Repeat with the remaining butter, then add the cayenne and a couple of good grinds of salt and pepper. Keep whisking the mixture until it is thick and creamy and forms a ribbon when you drizzle it back into the bowl.

4. Remove the sauce from the heat, cover with plastic wrap and set aside.

5. To poach the eggs, heat a medium pot filled with 5cm (2in) of water and the white vinegar until barely simmering – don't let it get beyond a simmer at any time.

6. Crack an egg into a small shallow saucer. Whisk the water to create a gentle whirlpool then gently slide the egg off the saucer into the middle of the whirlpool.

7. Cook for 3-4 minutes until set on the outside. Gently lift out of the saucepan with a slotted spoon, drain on some paper towels then place on one of the bowls. Repeat with the second egg.

8. Toast the bread slices, place two slices of salmon on each and divide between two serving plates. Top each slice with a poached egg, then pour over a generous amount of hollandaise.

9. Drizzle over a little bit of oil and garnish with micro greens.

HERB AND FETA FRITTATA

INGREDIENTS

2 tbsps olive oil

4 medium eggs, room temperature

1 tbsp milk

1 garlic clove, crushed

Salt and pepper

1 large beefsteak tomato, sliced

40g (1 ½ oz) Greek feta

Handful fresh basil leaves

4 sprigs fresh thyme

2 tbsps fresh parsley leaves

METHOD

1. Preheat the oven to 190°C (375°F, Gas Mark 5).

2. Grease a cast iron or ovenproof frying pan with half the oil.

3. In a large bowl, whisk together the eggs, milk and garlic for 3 minutes until light and fluffy. Season with a couple of good grinds of salt and pepper.

4. Pour the egg mixture into the pan. Arrange the sliced tomatoes in the egg mix, pushing them down so they're briefly submerged in the egg.

5. Bake in the oven for around 10 minutes or until just set.

6. Remove the frittata and sprinkle over the feta, basil, thyme, and parsley. Drizzle with the remaining olive oil and serve.

MUSHROOM OMELETTE WRAP

INGREDIENTS

2 medium eggs,
room temperature

1 tbsp milk

Salt and pepper

½ tbsp butter

1½ cups (225g, 8oz)
sliced button mushrooms

½ cup (100g, 3½ oz)
tomato, chopped

1 tbsp fresh dill, chopped

¼ cup (30g, 1oz) Swiss
cheese, grated

METHOD

1. In a large bowl, whisk together the eggs and milk for 3 minutes until light and fluffy. Season with a couple of good grinds of salt and pepper.

2. Heat a medium non-stick frying pan over medium heat and melt half the butter.

3. Fry the mushrooms for 4 minutes until browned. Remove them from the pan to a bowl and set aside. Add the tomato and fry for 1 minute then toss through the mushrooms with the dill.

4. Heat the rest of the butter, swirling to coat the bottom of the pan with it. Pour in the egg mixture and cook for 3 minutes until the surface is nearly cooked.

5. Sprinkle over the cheese, then slip the omelette off the pan and onto a serving plate.

6. Spread the mushroom mix along the middle of the omelette and fold the sides over the top.

7. Serve warm.

KEDGEREE

INGREDIENTS

3 tbsps butter

1 medium onion, finely chopped

¼ tsp ground cardamom

¼ tsp turmeric

½ stick cinnamon

2 bay leaves

3 cups (450g, 1lb) long-grain rice (such as basmati or jasmine)

4 cups (1L, 2pt) GF fish stock (can use vegetable)

Salt and pepper

6 medium eggs

750g (1½ lb) boneless smoked salmon chunks

3 tbsps capers, drained

3 tbsps fresh chives, chopped

METHOD

1. Melt the butter in a large deep-sided saucepan over medium heat. Add the onion and fry for 5 minutes until softened and just starting to brown. Stir through the spices and bay leaves for 1 minute.

2. Add the rice and stir for 2 minutes until coated in butter and translucent. Stir through the stock and a pinch of salt.

3. Bring to a boil, stirring to ensure the rice isn't sticking, then reduce the heat to low, cover and simmer for 12 minutes.

4. Bring a large pot of water to the simmering point. Gently lower the eggs in and simmer for 8 minutes until they're almost hard boiled. Remove the eggs and place in a large bowl filled with cold water. Once cool enough to handle, shell the eggs and slice them in half.

5. Stir the salmon into the kedgeree and cook for 3 more minutes.

6. Remove the pan from the heat, tip into a large bowl and gently toss through the capers and chives. Season to taste.

7. Divide between six serving plates and top each with two egg halves.

DETOX SMOOTHIE

INGREDIENTS

1 medium frozen banana

1 kiwi fruit, peeled and roughly chopped

1 green apple, peeled and cored

2 handfuls baby spinach

2 cups (500ml, 1pt) coconut water

2 cups (300g, 10oz) ice cubes

¼ cup (60ml, 2fl oz) coconut milk

METHOD

1. Let the banana defrost for at least 30 minutes, then roughly chop.

2. Place all the ingredients into a blender.

3. Blend on high speed until all ingredients are combined and you have a thick, smooth texture.

4. Pour the smoothies into two large drinking glasses or mason jars and serve.

OVERNIGHT SMOOTHIE

INGREDIENTS

¾ cup (60g, 2oz)
GF rolled oats, plus
2 tbsps to garnish

1 cup (250ml, 8fl oz)
Greek yoghurt

2½ tbsps agave syrup

¼ tsp vanilla essence

1 cup (225g, 8oz)
pumpkin puree (see
recipe page 17)

METHOD

1. Mix together the oats, ⅔ cup yoghurt, 1½ tablespoons of agave and vanilla in a bowl. Cover and sit in the refrigerator overnight.

2. In the morning, stir in the rest of the yoghurt.

3. Mix the pumpkin puree and remaining agave together. Place in a small saucepan over medium heat and cook for 5 minutes.

4. Remove the puree from the heat and divide between two serving glasses.

5. Top each with half of the yoghurt and oats mixture.

6. Sprinkle over the extra oats and serve.

SERVES 2 ★ PREP 15MIN ★ COOK TIME 30MIN

HOMESTYLE BEANS AND EGGS

INGREDIENTS

2 tbsps olive oil

1 small onion, chopped

1 garlic clove, minced

1 red capsicum, finely diced

1 large carrot, finely diced

½ tsp smoked paprika

1 tsp ground cumin

¼ tsp cayenne pepper

1 x 400g (14oz) can cannellini beans, drained

1x 400g (14oz) can diced tomatoes

1 tbsp lemon juice

½ cup (125ml, 4fl oz) GF vegetable stock

Salt and pepper

2 eggs

2 tbsps parsley, chopped

METHOD

1. In medium frying pan heat the olive oil over medium-high heat.
2. Add the onion and garlic and cook for 5 minutes, stirring frequently until the onion is softened.
3. Add the capsicum, carrot and spices and cook for a further 8 minutes, until the capsicum has softened. Add the beans, tomatoes, lemon juice and stock, as well as a couple of good grinds of salt and pepper and stir through. Bring to the boil, then reduce heat and simmer, covered, for 20 minutes, stirring occasionally.
4. Make two wells in the mixture and crack an egg into each. Cook for 5 minutes over low heat uncovered, then a further 2 minutes covered until the eggs are set to how you like them.
5. Sprinkle the parsley over the top and serve.

LEMON JAM

INGREDIENTS

3 medium lemons

1 medium yellow grapefruit

4 cups (1L, 2pt) water

50g (2oz) powdered fruit pectin

4 cups (880g, 2lb) caster sugar

¼ tsp almond extract

METHOD

1. Peel the lemons and grapefruit. Remove any pith from the peel and cut peel into 3mm (⅛ in) strips, then chop into roughly 5mm (¼ in) lengths. Set aside the flesh.

2. In a heavy-based large saucepan over medium-high heat, mix together the peel and water and bring to a boil. Reduce heat to a simmer, cover and let the peel cook and soften for 5 minutes.

3. Trim off any pith from the fruit flesh, chop up the flesh and remove any pips and membranes. Stir the chopped lemon and grapefruit flesh into the saucepan with the peel.

4. Stir through the pectin and bring to a boil. Stir and gradually add the sugar. Reduce the heat to a simmer and stir for at least 5 minutes until the sugar has dissolved.

5. Sterilise enough jars to hold 3L (100fl oz) of jam. Pour the hot jam into the jars. Seal the jars and boil for 10 minutes, completely submerged. Carefully remove the jars and let them cool.

MAKES 2½ CUPS ★ PREP 20MIN (PLUS CHILLING)

ALMOND MILK

INGREDIENTS

1 cup (160g, 6oz) raw almonds

Pinch of salt

6 cups (1.5L, 50fl oz) filtered or bottled water

125g (4oz) ice

¼ tsp vanilla extract

METHOD

1. Place the almonds in a large bowl. Add a pinch of salt to the almonds and pour in enough of the water so that there's 3cm (1in) covering them.

2. Soak for at least 8 hours, preferably overnight, at room temperature.

3. Drain the almonds and rinse them, then place them in a blender with 1½ cups water and blend until smooth. Pour in ½ cup water and the ice and puree again.

4. Strain the pulp in a nut milk bag, squeezing frequently to extract as much liquid as you can. Discard the pulp and pour the liquid and the vanilla extract into a sealable container.

5. The almond milk is now ready to drink. Store up to 3 days in the refrigerator.

MAKES 10-12 ★ PREP 20min (PLUS CHILLING)

GRANOLA BARS

INGREDIENTS

2½ cups (220g, 8oz)
GF rolled oats

⅔ cup (80g, 3oz)
cashews

½ cup (60g, 2oz) almonds

¾ cup (235g, 8oz) pure
maple syrup

½ cup (125g, 4oz) almond
butter (you can use GF
peanut butter)

½ cup (80g, 3oz) dried
cranberries, chopped

½ cup (80g, 3oz) sultanas

½ cup (60g, 2oz) dried
apple, roughly chopped

¼ cup (25g, 1oz)
goji berries, roughly
chopped

Pinch of salt

METHOD

1. Heat a large frying pan to medium-high and lightly toast the oats, cashews and almonds for 4 minutes.

2. Remove from the pan and into a large bowl.

3. In a separate bowl, beat together the maple syrup and almond butter.

4. Add the maple mix into the large bowl with the oat mixture and also add the rest of the ingredients.

5. Stir everything thoroughly so that all ingredients are combined. If it's too dry, add some more maple syrup.

6. Line an 18 x 28 cm (7 x 11in) slice tin with baking paper and pour the granola mix into the pan. Press it into the pan firmly and evenly.

7. Place in the refrigerator for at least 4 hours.

8. Cut into desired bar shapes and store in an airtight container. Will keep this way in the fridge for up to 2 weeks.

AMARANTH ENERGY BARS

INGREDIENTS

4 tbsps unsalted butter, chopped

¼ cup (40g, 1½ oz) palm sugar, grated

¼ cup (80g, 3oz) agave syrup

¼ tsp salt

½ tsp vanilla extract

1½ cups (35g, 1¼ oz) popped amaranth

1 cup (125g, 4oz) cashews, finely chopped

½ tbsp raw cacao powder

½ cup (85g, 3oz) Medjool dates, pitted, roughly chopped

½ cup (50g, 2oz) goji berries, roughly chopped

¼ cup (40g, 1½ oz) currants

METHOD

1. Preheat the oven to 160°C (325°F, Gas Mark 3) and line a 18 x 28 cm (7 x 11in) slice tin with baking paper.

2. Place the butter, sugar, agave and salt in a small saucepan over medium-high heat and stir until the butter is melted and the mixture is boiling.

3. Stir for about 4 minutes until it slightly thickens. Remove from heat.

4. Stir through the vanilla, remove to a large mixing bowl and stir in the rest of the ingredients.

5. Press into the baking dish in an even layer.

6. Bake for 10 minutes, then remove from the oven and let cool for 30 minutes.

7. Place in the refrigerator for at least 4 hours.

8. Cut into desired bar shapes and serve.

MAKES 12 ★ PREP 20min ★ COOK TIME 25min

PUMPKIN MUFFINS

INGREDIENTS

1 tbsp unsalted butter

1½ cups (260g, 9oz) Medjool dates, pitted and chopped

1 tsp allspice

1 large egg, room temperature

¾ cup (170g, 6oz) pumpkin puree (see recipe page 17)

1 cup (250ml, 8fl oz) milk

½ cup (80g, 3oz) brown sugar

¼ cup (20g, ¾ oz) desiccated coconut

2 tbsps canola oil

1 tsp vanilla extract

1½ cups (130g, 4½ oz) GF oat flour

1 tsp GF baking powder

½ tsp GF bicarbonate of soda

Pinch of salt

METHOD

1. Preheat the oven to 190°C (375°F, Gas Mark 5) and line two 6-hole muffin tins with muffin liners.

2. Heat the butter in a medium saucepan over medium heat. Stir in the dates and allspice and cook for 2 minutes. Remove from heat and set aside.

3. In a large mixing bowl, lightly whisk the egg, then stir through the pumpkin, milk, sugar, coconut, oil and vanilla. Ensure all ingredients are combined.

4. Sift the flour, baking powder and bicarb into the bowl and add a pinch of salt. Roughly mix through.

5. Spoon into the muffin liners and fill about three-quarters full. Bake for 23 minutes or until golden brown and a skewer inserted into the middle comes out clean.

6. Remove the muffins to a wire rack and let cool.

LIGHT
MEALS

SPICED CHICKPEA SOUP

INGREDIENTS

1 tbsp olive oil

1 small onion, finely chopped

2 medium carrots, diced

1 small celery stalk, with leaves, chopped

3 garlic cloves, crushed

2 cups (170g, 6oz) butternut pumpkin, cut into 1½ cm (¾ in) cubes

3 tbsps tomato paste

1 tsp cinnamon

1 tsp ground cumin

1 tsp ground coriander

½ tsp ground ginger

¼ tsp ground chilli

4 cups (1L, 2pt) GF vegetable stock

2 x 400g (14oz) cans chickpeas, rinsed and drained

1 cup (200g, 7oz) tomatoes, diced

½ cup (115g, 4oz) tomato passata

Salt and pepper

¼ cup (40g, 1½ oz) wild rice

½ tsp vegetable oil

Chives, to garnish

METHOD

1. Heat the oil in a large pot over medium-high heat. Add the onion, carrot and celery and saute for 5 minutes, stirring occasionally, until the onion is softened and starting to brown

2. Add the garlic and pumpkin and stir for 1 minute. Then stir through the tomato paste for another 1 minute to coat the vegetables.

3. Add the spices, stock, chickpeas, tomatoes and passata as well as a couple of good grinds of salt and pepper. Bring to a boil. Reduce the heat to a simmer and cook, covered, for 25 minutes.

4. While the soup is cooking, toast the rice. Heat the vegetable oil in a small frying pan over high heat. Add the rice, and shake the pan to coat the rice in the oil. Cover the pan and shake until you can hear rice popping. Reduce the heat to low and keep shaking until the popping slows down. Remove the rice immediately from the pan and set aside.

5. Season the soup to taste and serve, garnished with chives and popped wild rice.

PEA SOUP

INGREDIENTS

2 tbsps olive oil

2 tbsps unsalted butter

1 small onion, finely chopped

300g (10oz) potato, peeled and cut into 1cm (½ in) cubes

750g (1½ lb) fresh or frozen peas

¼ cup (10g, ¼ oz) fresh parsley, roughly chopped

Salt and pepper

3 cups (750ml, 24fl oz) GF chicken stock

1 cup (250ml, 8fl oz) cream

Parsley leaves, to garnish

METHOD

1. Heat the olive oil and half the butter in a large saucepan over medium heat. Add the onion and potato fry for 4 minutes until softened. Add the peas, parsley, a couple of good grinds of salt and pepper and cook for a further 8 minutes.

2. Add the chicken stock and bring to a boil. Reduce to a gentle simmer and cook, covered, for 10 minutes or until the potato is soft.

3. Place the soup in a blender in batches and puree until smooth.

4. Reheat until almost simmering and stir through the cream and the rest of the butter, stir for 2 minutes then remove from the heat. Season to taste.

5. Serve with a dash of extra cream and garnished with parsley leaves.

GRILLED CHICKEN BOWL

INGREDIENTS

¼ cup (60ml, 2fl oz) plus 1 tsp olive oil

2 garlic cloves, crushed

1 tbsp mixed herbs

1 tbsp GF tamari sauce

¼ tsp crushed chilli flakes

800g (1¾ lb) chicken breasts, skin removed

2 tbsps freshly squeezed lime juice

½ cup (65g, 2oz) pepitas (pumpkin seeds)

1 cup (155g, 4oz) medium-or long-grain brown rice

2 cups (500ml, 1pt) water

Pinch of salt

3 cups (225g, 8oz) broccoli florets

2 large avocados, sliced

½ cup (20g, ¾ oz) micro greens

METHOD

1. In a small mixing bowl, mix together the ¼ cup oil, garlic, herbs, tamari and chilli flakes. Pat the chicken breasts dry with paper towels and place in a container that fits them snugly and has a lid. Drizzle with the marinade, ensuring the chicken breasts are coated all over. Then sprinkle the lime juice over the top. Seal the container and place in the refrigerator for at least 1 hour to marinate.

2. To toast the pepitas, preheat a small frying pan over medium-high heat. Dry fry the pepitas for about 3 minutes or until they start to brown. Remove them immediately from the pan and set aside.

3. To cook the rice, first rinse the rice then drain it. Heat the 1 tsp olive oil in medium saucepan over medium-high heat and add the rice. Stir for 2 minutes, until the rice is slightly golden. Slowly add the water to the saucepan and stir through a pinch of salt. Bring the water to a boil, then reduce the heat to barely simmering and cook, covered, for 45 minutes. Don't remove the lid during this time.

4. Check the rice at the end of the 45 minutes, the water should be pretty much all absorbed. Remove from the heat and let sit, with the lid on, for 10 minutes.

5. Steam the broccoli until just tender while you grill the chicken.

6. Heat a grill pan or barbecue plate to high heat. Grill the chicken for 8 minutes each side or until cooked completely all the way through. Pour over any marinade that is left in the container.

7. Sit the breasts for 5 minutes before cutting into 1cm (½ in) thick slices.

8. To assemble, divide the rice between your serving bowls, place a quarter of the steamed broccoli on the side, arrange even portions of chicken on the rice, as well as slices of avocado. Sprinkle with toasted pepitas and some micro greens.

CHICKEN AND CAULIFLOWER MINI CASSEROLES

INGREDIENTS

2 tbsps olive oil

1 small onion, finely chopped

1 large garlic clove, crushed

6 chicken thigh fillets, skin removed, cut into 3cm (1in) cubes

½ medium head cauliflower, cut into small florets

100g (3½ oz) cream cheese, roughly chopped, room temperature

⅓ cup (100ml, 3½ fl oz) cream

4 spring onions, chopped

Salt and pepper

3 cups (90g, 3oz) baby spinach leaves, roughly chopped

¾ cup (100g, 3½ oz) tasty cheese, grated

1 cup (100g, 3½ oz) Parmesan cheese, grated

METHOD

1. Preheat the oven to 180°C (350°F, Gas Mark 4).

2. Heat half the oil a large frying pan over medium-high heat. Add the onion and fry for 5 minutes until softened and browned. Add the garlic and fry for a further minute.

3. Add the chicken and cook for 5 minutes until the chicken is just cooked. Remove from the pan into a large mixing bowl.

4. Steam the cauliflower for 4 minutes then add to the mixing bowl. Add the cream cheese, cream, spring onions and a couple of good grinds of salt and pepper. Toss to combine.

5. Divide the mixture between four large mini casserole dishes or 6 small ones.

6. Sprinkle over equal amounts of the spinach, then the two cheeses.

7. Bake for 15 minutes until the cheese is melted and browned.

PECAN-CRUSTED CHICKEN BREAST

INGREDIENTS

4 small boneless chicken breasts, skin removed

Crust

1½ cups (185g, 6oz) pecans

½ cup (40g, 1½ oz) desiccated coconut

½ tsp crushed chilli flakes

1 tbsp parsley, finely chopped

Salt and pepper

1 egg

Cucumber salad, to serve

METHOD

1. Preheat the oven to 200°C (400°F, Gas Mark 6) and line a baking dish with baking paper.

2. Place half the pecans in a blender and pulse until a fine crumb forms. Transfer to a mixing bowl and add the coconut, chilli, parsley, salt and pepper. Stir to combine and set aside.

3. Pulse remaining pecans to form a coarse crumble. Set aside.

4. Whisk the egg in a small bowl.

5. Coat each chicken breast in the ground pecan mixture, shaking off any excess. Dip in egg and shake off any excess. Then generously roll in the coarsely chopped pecans, shaking off any excess. Place the chicken breasts on the prepared baking tray.

6. Bake for 30-35 minutes until chicken is cooked through and the crust is golden. Remove from the oven and let sit for 5 minutes before slicing. Serve with cucumber salad.

MINI SPINACH AND EGG PIES

INGREDIENTS

Crust

3 cups (390g, 14oz) brown rice flour

½ tsp GF baking powder

1 tsp salt

90g (3oz) unsalted butter, chilled, cut into 1cm (½ in) cubes

2 small eggs, lightly beaten, room temperature

4 tbsps milk

Filling

1 tbsp olive oil

1 medium onion, finely chopped

1 garlic clove, crushed

4 cups (120g, 4oz) packed baby spinach, chopped

200g (7oz) creamy ricotta

¾ cup (100g, 3oz) tasty cheese, grated

Salt and pepper

Pinch of nutmeg

4 large eggs, room temperature

METHOD

1. Preheat the oven to 200°C (400°F, Gas Mark 6) and grease four 10cm tart tins with removable bottoms.

2. To make the crust, briefly pulse the flour, baking powder and salt a couple of times in a food processor. Add the butter and pulse a few times until the mixture resembles breadcrumbs. Mix the eggs together with the milk and slowly add to the mixture. Pulse until it begins to come together.

3. Let it sit for 5 minutes, then turn out onto a lightly rice floured work surface and press into four flat discs. Break one into two pieces, making one piece slightly larger than the other. Roll the larger portion into a circle of 13cm (5in) diameter. Place in a tart tin and push up to slightly above the edges. Repeat with the other pieces of dough. Fill the tarts with foil and baking beads and blind bake for 10 minutes. Remove the beads and bake for another 5 minutes. Remove and let cool.

4. To make the filling, heat the oil in a large saucepan over medium-high heat. Add the onion and fry for 5 minutes until softened and browned. Add the garlic and fry for a further minute. Add the spinach and stir through for 3 minutes until it is just starting to wilt. Tip the spinach mixture into a large mixing bowl.

5. Add the ricotta, cheese, a couple of good grinds of salt and pepper and the nutmeg and stir everything through.

6. Divide evenly between the four pie cases. Make a shallow well in each. Break an egg over each pie.

7. Roll out the remaining four pieces of pastry to fit on top of the pies. Press into the edges of the cooked pastry and prick lightly with a fork.

8. Bake the pies for 40 minutes until the pastry is golden brown.

9. Stand for 5 minutes before removing the pies from the tins.

SPINACH AND HERB GRATIN

INGREDIENTS

1 cup (250ml, 8fl oz) thickened cream

1 cup (250ml, 8fl oz) milk

140g (5oz) cream cheese, room temperature, cut into cubes

1¼ tsps salt

1 tbsp olive oil

1 large onion, chopped

3 garlic cloves, crushed

2-3 tbsps fresh parsley, finely chopped

1 tsp dried thyme

1 tsp dried basil

500g (1lb 2oz) fresh or frozen spinach, finely chopped

800g (1¾ lb) potatoes (such as Nicola or pontiac) peeled and grated and squeezed to remove some liquid

Pepper, to taste

1½ cups (175g, 6oz) tasty cheese, grated

METHOD

1. Preheat the oven to 200°C (400°F, Gas Mark 6) and grease a large deep-sided baking dish.

2. Add the cream, milk, cream cheese and salt to a medium saucepan over medium heat. Stir for 10 minutes until the cream cheese has melted and the sauce is smooth. Don't let the mixture boil. Remove from the heat.

3. Heat the oil in a medium frying pan and add the onion. Fry for 5 minutes until softened and translucent. Add the garlic and fry for a further minute, then transfer the onion and garlic to a large mixing bowl.

4. Add the parsley, dried herbs, spinach and potato and stir to combine along with a couple of good grinds of pepper.

5. Spread the spinach mixture over the bottom of the baking dish. Pour the warm cheese mixture over the top. Sprinkle over the tasty cheese.

6. Bake for 45 minutes until the mixture is set and the cheese on the top is browned and bubbling. Let rest for 10 minutes before serving.

SERVES 4 ★ PREP 10MIN ★ COOK TIME 30MIN

BANH XEO

INGREDIENTS

1 cup (250ml, 8fl oz) coconut milk

1¼ cups (125g, 4oz) rice flour

¼ cup (30g, 1oz) arrowroot flour

2 cups (500ml, 1pt) water, chilled

2 tbsps peanut oil

Pinch of ground turmeric

500g (1lb 2oz) cooked prawns talls, peeled

250g (9oz) fresh bean sprouts, rinsed and drained

1 cup (45g, 1½ oz) onion chives, cut into 3cm (1in) lengths

Sweet chilli sauce, to taste

METHOD

1. In a medium mixing bowl, whisk together the coconut milk, rice flour, arrowroot flour, water and half the oil until well mixed. Let sit for 30 minutes.

2. Heat a dash of the remaining oil in a medium (25cm/10in) non-stick frying pan over medium-high heat. Add the prawns and bean sprouts and quickly toss for 2 minutes then remove them from the pan and set aside.

3. Wipe down the frying pan then add the rest of the oil and heat over medium-high heat.

4. Give the batter a quick stir then pour ¼ cup of the batter into the frying pan and swirl until the whole pan is coated.

5. Cook the crepe for about 5 minutes until the underside is golden. Place a small portion of prawns, sprouts and chives on half the crepe, then fold the other half over.

6. Transfer to a serving dish. Repeat with the rest of the batter, and serve with sweet chilli sauce on the side.

MUSHROOM QUICHE

INGREDIENTS

Base

½ cup (65g, 2oz) arrowroot flour

½ cup (45g, 1½ oz) chickpea flour

⅓ cup (45g, 1½ oz) rice flour

½ tsp salt

115g (4oz) unsalted butter, cubed, chilled

3 tbsps cold water

Filling

3 tbsps olive oil

2 leeks, thinly sliced

4 cups (600g, 1lb 5oz) mixed mushrooms, sliced

⅓ cup (45g, 1½ oz) arrowroot flour

2 cups (250g, 8oz) Swiss cheese, grated

¼ cup (60ml, 2fl oz) GF mirin

1 tsp dried oregano

Pinch of allspice

Salt and pepper

1 cup (250ml, 8fl oz) milk

1 cup (250ml, 8fl oz) thickened cream

3 medium eggs, lightly beaten, room temperature

Parsley, to garnish

METHOD

1. To make the base, place the flours, salt and butter in a food processor and pulse a few times until it resembles breadcrumbs. Add the water in small amounts until the mixture comes together to form a dough. You may need more or less water.

2. Remove the mixture and form it into a round flattened disc. Wrap in plastic wrap and place in the refrigerator for at least 30 minutes to chill.

3. Preheat the oven to 190°C (375°F, Gas Mark 5) and lightly grease a 27cm (10½ in) quiche tin with a removable bottom.

4. Roll out the dough onto a lightly floured surface into a circles about 30cm (12in) diameter. Place into the tin and press into the sides. Prick the bottom with a fork. Line with foil and fill with baking beads or uncooked rice.

5. Bake for 20 minutes, then remove the foil and beads and set aside.

6. To make the filling, heat the oil in a large saucepan over medium-high heat. Add the leek and fry for 5 minutes until softened and browned. Add the mushrooms and fry for a further 5 minutes. Stir through the flour and cook for 1 minute.

7. Transfer the mushroom mix to a large mixing bowl and stir in the cheese, mirin, oregano, allspice and a couple of good grinds of salt and pepper. In another bowl whisk together the milk, cream and eggs. Pour the wet ingredients into the mushroom mixture and mix thoroughly.

8. Pour the mushroom mix into the quiche case and bake for 35 minutes, until the quiche is set. Let cool for a few minutes before removing from the baking tin.

9. Serve garnished with parsley.

RICE CROQUETTE

INGREDIENTS

Filling

2 cups (330g, 12oz) cooked and cooled short-grain rice

⅓ cup (30g, 1oz) Parmesan cheese, grated

¼ cup (30g, 1oz) mozzarella, grated

1 large egg, lightly beaten, room temperature

Salt and pepper

Crumb coating

1 large egg, lightly beaten, room temperature

1 cup (125g, 4oz) GF breadcrumbs

½ tsp salt

¼ tsp pepper

3 tbsps canola oil

1 tbsp fresh parsley, roughly chopped

METHOD

1. Place the all the filling ingredients including a good couple of grinds of salt and pepper together in a large mixing bowl.

2. Use your hands to mix everything together thoroughly and then shape into 10 rounds balls.

3. Place the egg in a shallow bowl and the breadcrumbs and salt and pepper in another.

4. Dip each ball into the egg, then coat in the crumbs until coated.

5. Heat the oil in a shallow frying pan over medium-high heat. Place a few croquettes in the pan and push down gently to flatten them slightly.

6. Fry for 3 minutes on each side or until the breadcrumbs are golden.

7. Drain on paper towels and repeat with the rest of the croquettes.

8. Serve hot, sprinkled with parsley.

GREEN RISOTTO

INGREDIENTS

3 tbsps olive oil

1 medium onion, finely chopped

400g (14oz) fresh or frozen peas

¼ cup (5g, ¼ oz) loosely packed mint leaves, plus sprigs to garnish

3 tbsps unsalted butter

1 garlic clove, crushed

2 cups (320g, 11oz) Arborio rice

2¼ cups (560ml, 19 fl oz) white wine

4 cups (1L, 2pt) GF chicken stock

⅓ cup (40g, 1½ oz) Romano cheese, finely grated

Salt and pepper

METHOD

1. Heat 1 tablespoon of oil in a small saucepan over medium-high heat. Add half the onion and fry for 3 minutes until softened. Add the peas and a couple of tablespoons of water. Cover and cook on low heat for 6 minutes or until cooked. Remove from the heat and let cool. Place in a blender with the mint leaves and blend into a smooth puree. Set aside.

2. Heat the rest of the oil with 1 tablespoon of butter in a large, deep-sided frying pan over medium-high heat. Add the rest of the onion and fry for 5 minutes until softened and browned. Add the garlic and rice and stir for 2 minutes until the rice is translucent.

3. Pour in the wine and let it cook off for 1 minute. Gradually add the chicken stock 1 cup at a time, ensuring it's all absorbed by the rice before adding more. When stock is nearly absorbed and the rice is still slightly firm, stir in the pea puree, the rest of the butter and half the cheese. Cook for 5 minutes or until the rice is tender.

4. Season to taste and serve sprinkled with the remaining Romano and garnished with sprigs of mint.

SERVES 4 ★ PREP 20min ★ COOK TIME 25min

SPAGHETTI SQUASH WITH SATAY SAUCE

INGREDIENTS

2 large spaghetti squash

2 tbsps salt

2 cups (300g, 10oz) sweet potato, peeled and cubed

¾ cup (185g, 6oz) GF peanut butter (can use almond or cashew)

2 tbsps fresh ginger, minced

2 garlic cloves, crushed

3 tbsps GF tamari sauce

2 tbsps lime juice

2 tbsps fresh Thai basil, finely chopped

½ cup (60g, 2oz) dry roasted peanuts, finely chopped

1 medium red chilli, seeded and roughly chopped

Fresh basil leaves, to garnish

METHOD

1. Preheat the oven to 200°C (400°F, Gas Mark 6) and line a large baking tray with baking paper.

2. Cut the squash in half width-wise and remove the seeds.

3. Rub the squash with salt and sit on a wire rack over the baking dish, cut side underneath to let the liquid drain away. Wipe off the salt after 20 minutes, remove the baking paper and bake squash for 25 minutes. Let cool for 10 minutes then use a fork to gently shred into strands for the spaghetti into a large mixing bowl.

4. While the squash is baking, make the sauce so it's ready at the same time as the spaghetti.

5. Boil the sweet potato in 2 cups of water for 5 minutes until tender. Drain the potatoes, but reserve the water they boiled in. Let the potato cool for 5 minutes then place in a blender with the peanut butter, ginger, garlic, tamari, lime, basil and peanuts. Blend into a smooth puree, adding water as needed to make it a sauce. Season to taste.

6. Pour the sauce over the hot spaghetti and toss together.

7. Serve hot topped with chilli and basil leaves.

QUINOA SALAD WITH CRANBERRIES AND KALE

INGREDIENTS

2 cups (340g, 12oz) uncooked quinoa

4 cups (1L, 2pt) GF vegetable stock

¾ cup (90g, 3oz) slivered almonds

10 cups (700g, 1½ lb) raw kale, stems removed and chopped

¾ cup (120g, 4oz) dried cranberries

Dressing

¼ cup (60ml, 2fl oz) lemon juice

1 tsp Dijon mustard

¼ cup (60ml, 2fl oz) olive oil

1 clove garlic, minced

1 tbsp honey

Salt and pepper

METHOD

1. Rinse the quinoa and put into a large saucepan with the stock. Bring to a boil, then reduce the heat to low, cover and cook for 15 minutes or until the quinoa is cooked. Stir occasionally to ensure the quinoa isn't sticking to the bottom of the pot. Once cooked, transfer to a large mixing bowl to cool for 15 minutes.

2. In a small frying pan, dry-fry the slivered almonds over high heat for 2 minutes or until they start to brown. Add immediately to the quinoa.

3. Add the kale and cranberries to the bowl and toss together.

4. In a small bowl, vigorously whisk together the dressing ingredients.

5. Pour the dressing over the salad and toss everything together to thoroughly coat the quinoa and kale.

6. Season to taste with salt and pepper and serve.

KALE AND TURKEY EGG MUFFINS

INGREDIENTS

10 large eggs,
room temperature

1 tbsp olive oil

1 medium onion,
finely chopped

250g (9oz) minced
turkey breast

2 cups (270g, 9oz)
chopped kale leaves,
stems removed

Salt and pepper, to taste

¼ cup (10g, ¼ oz)
micro greens, to garnish

METHOD

1. Preheat the oven to 190°C (375°F, Gas Mark 5) and lightly oil 12 muffin tin holes.

2. Whisk the eggs together in a large bowl and set aside.

3. Heat the oil in a large saucepan over medium-high heat. Add the onion and fry for 4 minutes until softened. Add the turkey and cook for 5 minutes, breaking up into small pieces with a wooden spoon. Reduce heat to medium and add kale leaves in small batches, stirring until wilted. Season with salt and pepper.

4. Divide turkey mix between the muffin holes, then pour egg over the top of each to about 1cm (½ in) below the top of the muffin hole.

5. Bake for 20 minutes or until the muffins are completely set.

6. Serve warm, garnished with micro greens.

STUFFED CABBAGE LEAVES

INGREDIENTS

Sauce

1 tsp olive oil

1 onion, finely chopped

Pinch of GF bicarbonate of soda

3 garlic cloves, crushed

1 x 800g (1¾ lb) can diced tomatoes

1 cup (200g, 7oz) passata

½ tbsp tomato paste

1 tsp salt

Pinch of ground chilli

Cabbage rolls

1 large white cabbage

3 cups (495g, 1lb 1oz) cooked long-grain rice

1 cup (200g, 7oz) just cooked sweet potato, finely chopped

1 medium onion, finely chopped

2 garlic cloves, crushed

2 tsps lemon juice

1 tsp smoky paprika

Salt and pepper, to taste

¼ tsp nutmeg

¼ cup (10g, ¼ oz) parsley, roughly chopped

METHOD

1. Heat the oil in a large frying pan over medium-high heat and add the onions and a pinch of bicarb. Fry onion for 5 minutes. Add garlic and cook for a further minute. Add the rest of the sauce ingredients, stir, reduce the heat to low and simmer, covered, for at least 35 minutes.

2. Fill a deep pot with water and bring the water to a boil. Remove any damaged outer leaves from the cabbage, and cut out as much of the core as possible. Place cabbage upside down in the pot. Boil until the leaves start to soften and separate. Use a sharp knife and tongs to carefully remove 12 whole cabbage leaves.

3. Place the leaves and the remaining cabbage head in a strainer and rinse under cold water. Finely shred the cabbage (apart from the leaves) and add it to the simmering sauce. Keep the sauce covered and continue to cook on very low.

4. Place the rice, sweet potato, onion, garlic, lemon juice, paprika, salt and pepper and nutmeg in a large mixing bowl and mix through until thoroughly combined. Season further to taste.

5. Pat dry each cabbage leaf before using and trim off the thick stem. Place a heaped ¼ cup of the stuffing in the middle of the leaf. Fold the stem end up over the filling, fold the two sides over the filling and roll it up snugly. Place, rolled end side down, on a plate and repeat with the rest of the cabbage leaves.

6. Spread half the tomato sauce in the bottom of a large heavy-based pot. Fit the rolls snugly in a single layer on top of the sauce. Spoon over the rest of the sauce, cover and cook on low for 50 minutes.

7. Serve warm, garnished with chopped parsley.

FRUITY GOAT CHEESE SALAD

INGREDIENTS

3 medium beetroots, ends trimmed

2 tbsps olive oil

Salt and pepper

4 cups (120g, 4oz) mixed lettuce leaves

1 cup (75g, 3oz) radicchio leaves, torn

1 cup (200g, 7oz) fresh pineapple, cut into bite-size chunks

²/₃ cup (80g, 3oz) cashews

⅓ cup (75ml, 2½ fl oz) balsamic vinegar

120g (4oz) goat cheese, crumbled

METHOD

1. Preheat the oven to 180°C (350°F, Gas Mark 4).

2. Place each beetroot in a large square of foil, large enough to wrap it up completely in.

3. Drizzle ½ teaspoon olive oil over each beetroot and season with salt and pepper. Wrap them up and bake in the oven for 50 minutes until tender.

4. Let them cool for 20 minutes before peeling – the skin should peel off easily with your fingers.

5. Halve and slice the beetroots and place in a large mixing bowl with the lettuce, radicchio, pineapple and cashews.

6. Pour over the rest of the olive oil and the balsamic vinegar along with a couple of good grinds of salt and pepper.

7. Divide the salad between serving plates and sprinkle over the goat cheese to serve.

COCONUT PRAWN TEMPURA

INGREDIENTS

24 prawn tails, ends intact

Batter

1 large egg, beaten

²/₃ cup (160ml, 5fl oz) coconut milk.

¾ cup (100g, 3½ oz) arrowroot flour

1½ tsps GF baking powder

Coating

½ cup (65g, 2oz) arrowroot flour, divided

2 cups (180g, 6oz) shredded coconut

Coconut oil, melted, for frying

METHOD

1. Line a large flat tray with baking paper and set aside.

2. In a mixing bowl, whisk together the egg, coconut milk, arrowroot flour and baking powder to form a smooth batter.

3. In a separate bowl, mix together ¼ cup of arrowroot flour and the shredded coconut. Place on a flat plate and set aside.

4. Place remaining ¼ cup of arrowroot flour in a shallow bowl.

5. Holding a prawn by the tail, lightly coat in flour, shaking off any excess. Dip in the batter, again shaking to remove excess. Then roll the prawn in the coconut mix. Place the coated prawn on the tray and repeat with the rest of the prawns.

6. Pour 4cm (1½ in) of oil into a pan and heat over medium-high heat. Drop a small amount of the batter mix into the oil and when it bubbles and rises, the oil is ready to cook with.

7. Carefully place 2-3 prawns in the oil and fry for 3 minutes or until golden. Use a metal slotted spoon to remove and drain on paper towels. Repeat with the rest of the prawns.

VEGETARIAN PIZZA ON SWEET POTATO CRUST

INGREDIENTS

Crust

1 medium uncooked sweet potato, peeled

1 medium egg, lightly beaten

Pinch of GF onion powder

½ tsp salt

⅔ cup (60g, 2oz) GF rolled oats

1 tbsp olive oil

Topping

½ cup (75g, 3oz) button mushrooms, sliced

1 small red onion, thinly sliced

6 cherry tomatoes, halved

6 small bocconcini, halved

2 tbsps flat-leaf parsley, roughly chopped

METHOD

1. Preheat the oven to 200°C (400°F, Gas Mark 6) and line a pizza tray with baking paper.

2. Pulse the sweet potato through a food processor until broken up into small pieces. Add the egg, onion powder and salt and pulse again to mix through a few times. The mixture should resemble a thick paste Add the oats and again pulse a couple times until it looks like a batter.

3. Tip out onto the baking tray and press out into a pizza base around 5mm (¼ in) thick. Bake for 25 minutes until slightly browned and dried out on top. Remove and let cool for 15 minutes. Carefully flip the base over, then peel off the paper. Brush with the oil and bake for a further 10 minutes.

4. Arrange the mushrooms, onion and tomatoes on the base. Top with the bocconcini and reduce the oven to 180°C (350°F, Gas Mark 4). Bake for 10-15 minutes or until the cheese has melted.

5. Sprinkle with parsley, cut into slices and serve hot.

BBQ CHICKEN PIZZA ON POLENTA CRUST

INGREDIENTS

Crust

4 cups (1L, 2pt) water

1 cup (160g, 6oz) polenta

1 tbsp olive oil

1 tsp salt

2 tbsps grated Parmesan

1 cup (125g, 4oz) cooked shredded chicken

1 small red onion, thinly sliced

½ cup (20g, ¾ oz) shredded basil leaves

2 tbsps GF barbecue sauce

METHOD

1. Line a baking tray with lightly oiled baking paper and set aside.

2. Bring the water to a boil in a large saucepan. Stir with a whisk and slowly pour in the polenta in a fine stream. Reduce heat to low and add the half the oil and the salt. Whisk continuously for 30 minutes until the polenta starts to come away from the sides of the saucepan. Stir in the Parmesan and remove from the heat.

3. Using a spatula, spread the polenta in a smooth circle on the tray about 5mm (¼ in) thick. Cover with oiled plastic wrap, place in the refrigerator for up to 4 hours, or overnight.

4. Preheat oven to 230°C (450°F, Gas Mark 8). Drizzle oil over crust and bake for 15 minutes until crispy at edges. Remove from oven.

5. Top the base with the chicken and onion and bake for 15 minutes. Scatter the basil leaves over the top and drizzle over the barbecue sauce. Serve hot.

CHILLI POTATO PIZZA ON GLUTEN-FREE CRUST

METHOD

1. Preheat the oven to 230°C (450°F, Gas Mark 8) and line a pizza (or baking) tray with oiled baking paper.

2. In a large mixing bowl, whisk together the flours, salt, yeast, and sugar. Pour over the warm water and stir with a fork until it starts to come together. Add more water as needed. Form into a ball, cover with a damp tea towel and let sit for 15 minutes. Press the dough onto the tray and shape it into a circle about 30cm (12in).

3. Bake for 12 minutes until golden brown.

4. Scatter over the grated carrot, then Parmesan. Arrange potato slices over the top then sprinkle with chilli and mozzarella.

5. Reduce the heat to 180°C (350°F, Gas Mark 4) and bake the pizza for 20 minutes or until the potato is cooked. Remove from the oven, sprinkle over the thyme and serve hot.

INGREDIENTS

Base

¾ cup (80g, 3oz) quinoa flour

¼ cup (35g, 1¼ oz) teff flour

¼ tsp salt

1 tsp dried yeast

½ tsp light brown sugar

½ cup (125ml, 4fl oz) warm water

1 tbsp olive oil

Toppings

1 small carrot, grated

¼ cup (25g, 1oz) Parmesan cheese

1 cup (225g, 8oz) thinly sliced potato (Desiree or Dutch cream)

2 tsps chilli flakes

⅓ cup (40g, 1½ oz) mozzarella, grated

2 tsps thyme leaves

MAKES 20 ★ PREP 40MIN ★ COOK TIME 40MIN

HOMEMADE CHICKEN NUGGETS AND KETCHUP

INGREDIENTS

Ketchup

¾ cup (180g, 6oz) tomato paste

½ cup (125ml, 4fl oz) apple cider vinegar

½ tsp Dijon mustard

½ cup (125ml, 4fl oz) water

½ tsp salt

½ tsp ground oregano

½ tsp ground cumin

Nuggets

500g (1lb 2oz) minced chicken

2 tbsps GF chicken stock

¾ tsp salt

¼ tsp mustard powder

¼ tsp onion powder

Coating

½ cup (45g, 1½ oz) chickpea flour

3 tbsps tapioca flour

½ tsp salt

¼ tsp GF baking powder

2 medium eggs, lightly beaten

½ cup (125ml, 4fl oz) soda water

Canola or vegetable oil

2 tbsps parsley, chopped

1 lemon, cut into wedges

METHOD

1. To make the ketchup, combine all the ingredients in a small saucepan and heat over medium-high heat until almost boiling. Reduce heat to low and simmer for 30 minutes until thickened. Season to taste and let cool before serving.

2. To make the nuggets, line two large flat trays with baking paper.

3. Place the chicken, stock, salt, mustard and onion powders in a mixing bowl and use your hands to mix until combined. Form large spoonfuls of the mixture into nugget shapes. Place them on one of the trays.

4. Mix together the chickpea flour, tapioca flour, salt and baking powder in a shallow bowl and stir to combine well.

5. Place the beaten eggs in a separate shallow bowl and whisk through the soda water.

6. Dip the nuggets in the egg mixture, then coat in the flour mixture and then place on the other baking tray.

7. Once finished, throw out the baking paper from the first tray and replace it with paper towels.

8. Pour 4cm (1½ in) of oil into a medium-sized pot and heat over medium-high heat. Drop a small amount of the coating mix into the oil and when it bubbles and rises, the oil is ready to cook with.

9. Carefully place a couple of nuggets in the oil and fry for 4 minutes or until golden. Use a metal slotted spoon to lift them out and drain them on the paper towels.

10. Repeat with the rest of the nuggets.

11. Serve them hot with the ketchup and lemon wedges.

CHICKEN SALAD WITH CREAMY RANCH DRESSING

INGREDIENTS

Dressing

1 cup (250ml, 8fl oz) almond milk (see recipe page 37)

½ cup (120g, 4oz) mayonnaise

1 tbsp apple cider vinegar

1 tbsp white chia seeds

2 tsps parsley, chopped

1 tsp dill, finely chopped

Salt and pepper

¼ tsp GF onion powder

Pinch of garlic powder

Salad

600g (1lb 5oz) chicken thigh, cut into bite-size pieces

1½ tbsps olive oil

2 garlic cloves, crushed

1 tbsp lime juice

1 tbsp seeded mustard

1 cup (175g, 6oz) fresh corn kernels

4 cups (125g, 4oz) baby spinach leaves

2 medium avocados, cubed

2 large oranges, peeled and sliced, seeds removed

1 cup (100g, 3½ oz) pomegranate seeds

METHOD

1. To make the dressing, tip all the ingredients into a blender or food processor and process until smooth. Transfer to a sealable container and keep in the refrigerator until needed.

2. Place the chicken in a mixing bowl with the oil, garlic, lime juice and mustard and toss to coat the chicken.

3. Heat a large frying pan over medium-high heat and fry the chicken pieces for 8 minutes, until cooked through. Remove from heat and place in a large mixing bowl.

4. Add the corn to the pan and stir for 5 minutes until the kernels are cooked. Place the corn into the bowl with the chicken and let sit for 10 minutes to cool down.

5. Add the spinach leaves, avocado, orange slices and pomegranate seeds and gently toss to combine.

6. Divide the salad between four serving plates and drizzle with the ranch dressing. Serve.

LEMON PARSLEY MUSSELS WITH SALSA VERDE

INGREDIENTS

Salsa verde

1½ cups (65g, 2oz) flat-leaf parsley, roughly chopped

½ cup (20g, ¾ oz) fresh mint, roughly chopped

¼ cup (10g, ¼ oz) fresh dill, roughly chopped

2 anchovy fillets

1 garlic clove, chopped

1 tbsp capers, rinsed and drained

½ tsp caster sugar

Salt and pepper

1 tbsp white wine vinegar

½ cup (125ml, 4fl oz) olive oil

Mussels

1kg (2lb) fresh mussels, scrubbed and debearded

1 tbsp butter

½ cup (125ml, 4fl oz) dry white wine

½ cup (125ml, 4fl oz) GF chicken stock

⅓ cup (15g, ½ oz) flat-leaf parsley, roughly chopped

Lemon wedges, to serve

METHOD

1. Add the herbs, anchovies, garlic, capers, sugar and a couple of good grinds of salt and pepper to a blender or use a stick blender to combine. Then add the vinegar and start to drizzle in the oil, while blending. You want a nice green, rough sauce, not a puree. Season to taste, then transfer the sauce to a small serving bowl and set aside.

2. Sit the mussels in a large container of fresh water about 15 minutes before cooking.

3. Melt the butter in a large pot with a lid over medium heat. When the butter begins to foam, add the white wine, stock and mussels. Put the lid on and cook the mussels for about 8 minutes, giving the pot a good shake every 2 minutes.

4. Divide the mussels between two large serving bowls and place a large 'discard' bowl on the table as well.

5. Serve the mussels with parsley scattered over and salsa verde and lemon wedges on the side.

SOY AND SESAME BAKED EGGPLANT

INGREDIENTS

¼ cup (70g, 2½ oz) white miso paste

1 tbsp rice wine vinegar

2 tbsps GF tamari sauce

1 tbsp water

1 tbsp fresh ginger, minced

1 garlic clove, crushed

1 tbsp pure maple syrup

2 large eggplants, halved

2 tbsps sesame oil

1½ tbsps sesame seeds

2 spring onions, thinly sliced on the diagonal, to garnish

1 tbsp parsley leaves, to garnish

METHOD

1. Whisk together the miso, vinegar, tamari, water, ginger, garlic and maple syrup in a medium bowl.

2. Use a sharp, pointed knife to cut cross-hatches into the eggplant, cutting the flesh all the way through to the skin but don't cut the skin.

3. Drizzle the sesame oil over the cut halves of the eggplants and gently rub it into the cuts.

4. Heat a large non-stick frying pan over medium-high heat. Place the eggplants on it, cut side up, and fry for 3 minutes, until the underside is slightly charred. Turn them over and cook for 5 minutes, until the flesh is softened and mushy, then gently and carefully remove them remove from the pan.

5. Line a deep-sided baking dish with baking paper and place the halves on it, cut side up.

6. Heat a grill to high.

7. Brush a third of the sauce over each eggplant and place them under the grill.

8. Cook for 3 minutes until the sauce is caramelised and browned. Brush the tops of the eggplant again with the rest of the sauce and cook for 2 further minutes.

9. Serve them hot sprinkled with sesames seeds, spring onion and a couple of parsley leaves.

SERVES 4-8 ★ PREP 20MIN ★ COOK TIME 4HR (OR LONGER)

PERUVIAN SCALLOPS

INGREDIENTS

500g (1lb 2oz) fresh
scallops with beards

1 cup (225g, 8oz) cherry
tomatoes

1 cup (175g, 6oz) cooked
corn kernels

1 small red onion

1 medium red chilli,
seeded and finely chopped

¼ cup (10g, ¼ oz) fresh
coriander, finely chopped,
plus extra for garnish

1 cup (250ml, 8fl oz)
fresh orange juice

⅓ cup (80ml, 3fl oz)
fresh lemon juice

⅓ cup (80ml, 3fl oz)
fresh lime juice

2 tbsps coconut milk

8 scallop shells

Salt, to taste

Lemon slices, to garnish

METHOD

1. Chop the scallops into small cubes, about 7mm (¼ in) wide. Chop
    the tomatoes into the same size and finely chop the red onion.

2. Combine all the ingredients except the shells, salt and lemon slices
    in a large glass (non-reactive) bowl and stir to ensure the scallop
    meat is coated in citrus juice.

3. Cover the bowl and place in the refrigerator for at least 4 hours,
    preferably overnight, to cook.

4. Dip the scallop shells into boiling water for 1 minute before use.

5. Season the scallop mix to taste with salt, then divide it between the
    shells.

6. Sprinkle over the extra coriander and serve with lemon slices on the
    side.

MUSHROOM BURGER

INGREDIENTS

1 tbsp olive oil

1 tbsp GF tamari sauce

1 garlic clove, minced

1 tsp salt

4 large portobello mushrooms, wiped clean and stems removed

1 avocado

1 tsp lime juice

Salt and pepper

1 large tomato, cut into thick slices

Handful mixed salad leaves, washed and dried

¼ cup (60ml, 2fl oz) sour cream

2 tsps sesame seeds

METHOD

1. Preheat oven to 190°C (375°F, Gas Mark 5). Line a large flat baking tray with baking paper.

2. Mix together the oil, tamari, garlic and salt. Lightly coat each mushroom in the mixture and place them upside-down on the baking tray.

3. Roast for 10 minutes, then turn them over and roast for a further 15 minutes. Remove them from the tray and let them sit on paper towels to help remove some of the excess liquid.

4. Mash the avocado together with the lime juice and salt and pepper to taste.

5. To assemble, place two mushrooms upside-down on your serving plates. Spread half the avocado onto each mushroom.

6. Top with a slice or two of tomato, then some salad leaves, then a good dollop of sour cream.

7. Top with the other mushroom half and sprinkle them with the sesame seeds.

MAIN MEALS

FENNEL ROASTED MACKEREL AND VEGETABLES

INGREDIENTS

400g (14oz) fresh mackerel fillets, skin on

2 tsps Dijon mustard

2 tbsps fresh rosemary leaves, chopped

2 large potatoes, peeled and cubed (use a good baking type such as Dutch cream or sebago)

1 large carrot, peeled, quartered and sliced

2 tbsps olive oil

Salt and pepper

50g (2oz) green beans, ends trimmed, cut into 3cm (1in) lengths

450g (1lb) fennel bulbs, sliced paper thin

2 shallots, peeled and finely sliced

3 tbsps dry white wine

Cherry tomatoes, to garnish

Lettuce leaves, to garnish

METHOD

1. Two hours before cooking, rinse and pat dry the fillets, then spread the Dijon mustard and 1 tablespoon rosemary over them. Cover and sit in the refrigerator until ready to cook.

2. Preheat the oven to 180°C (350°F, Gas Mark 4).

3. Toss the potatoes and carrot together with the rest of the rosemary, 1 tablespoon of the olive oil and a couple of good grinds of salt and pepper.

4. Place in a baking dish and bake for 20 minutes. Remove the tray from the oven, toss the green beans through and return to the oven for 25 minutes.

5. Toss together the fennel and shallots and spread them over the bottom of a small baking dish that will hold the fillets snugly. Drizzle the fennel mix with the rest of the olive oil and the wine and then place the fish on top. Bake for 20 minutes, then let sit, covered, for 5 minutes before serving.

6. Serve the fish on a small bed of fennel, with the baked vegetables on the side, garnished with fresh cherry tomatoes and salad leaves.

SALMON AND ASPARAGUS WITH CREAMY DILL SAUCE

INGREDIENTS

4 x 200g (7oz) salmon fillets

Salt and pepper

1 tbsp butter

20 medium asparagus spears

4 sprigs dill, to garnish

Lemon wedges, to garnish

Dill sauce

1½ tsps canola or vegetable oil

2 small garlic cloves, crushed

¼ cup (50ml, 2fl oz) dry white wine

¼ cup (50ml, 2fl oz) lemon juice

1½ tbsps dill, finely chopped

70g (2½ oz) unsalted butter, room temperature, cubed

Salt and pepper

½ tsp arrowroot flour

2 tbsps creme fraiche

METHOD

1. To make the sauce, heat the oil in a small saucepan over medium-low heat. Fry the garlic for 1 minute until fragrant but not browned. Stir in the white wine for 2 minutes, then add the lemon juice and dill and simmer for 2 more minutes.

2. Add the butter and gently stir while it melts. Season to taste with salt. Stir the arrowroot flour into the creme fraiche, then vigorously mix the creme fraiche into the sauce. Let it cook for another 2 minutes, season to taste, cover and set aside.

3. To cook the salmon, season the fillets with freshly ground salt and pepper then heat a frying pan over medium-high heat and melt the butter in it. Place the fish skin-side down and fry for 6 minutes. Then gently flip over and cook for another 5 or until the fillets are cooked to your preference.

4. Steam the asparagus for 5 minutes. Serve the salmon and asparagus drizzled with sauce and garnished with dill and lemon.

SERVES 4 ★ PREP 20MIN ★ COOK TIME 35MIN

COD WITH MEDITERRANEAN VEGETABLES

INGREDIENTS

2 large potatoes, peeled and cut into 5mm (¼ in) thick slices

2 cups (450g, 1lb) cherry tomatoes

2 tbsps olive oil

Salt and pepper

1 cup (140g, 5oz) Kalamata olives

1 cup (140g, 5oz) green olives

2 tsps red wine vinegar

¼ cup (10g, ¼ oz) fresh parsley, finely chopped

800g (1¾ lb) fresh rockling fillets, deboned

2 garlic cloves, crushed

Lemon wedges, to serve

METHOD

1. Preheat the oven to 200°C (400°F, Gas Mark 6) and line a baking tray with baking paper.

2. Toss the potato slices and tomatoes with ½ tablespoon olive oil and season with salt and pepper. Place on baking tray and transfer to oven to bake for 15 minutes. Remove from the oven and toss the olives through, then bake for another 10 minutes, until the potato slices are tender and golden.

3. Once cooked, remove the vegetables from the oven, place in a bowl, sprinkle the vinegar and a pinch of parsley over the top, gently toss, cover and let sit for 5 minutes before serving.

4. Heat the rest of the oil in a non-stick frying pan over medium-high heat. Rub the fish with the garlic and salt and pepper. Cook for 3 minutes each side or until cooked through.

5. Serve the fish on top of the vegetables, garnished with the rest of the parsley and lemon wedges on the side.

MILLET PUMPKIN BURGERS

INGREDIENTS

½ cup (100g, 3½ oz) dried millet

½ cup (90g, 3oz) yellow lentils

¾ cup (125g, 4oz) chickpeas, tinned or cooked

¾ cup (170g, 6oz) pumpkin puree (see recipe page 17)

¾ cup (125g, 4oz) tinned or cooked black beans, rinsed and drained

⅓ cup (30g, 1oz) GF rolled oats

½ tbsp olive oil

1 small onion, finely diced

2 garlic cloves, crushed

4-6 semi sun-dried tomatoes, finely chopped

1 tsp ground chilli powder

1 tsp turmeric

1 tsp smoky paprika

2 tsps ground oregano

1 tbsp Dijon mustard

¼ cup (25g, 1oz) coconut flour

¼ cup (10g, ¼ oz) fresh basil leaves, shredded

1 large egg, lightly beaten

Salt and pepper

Olive oil, for frying

METHOD

1. The night before, soak the millet in 1 cup of water.

2. To make the burgers, drain the millet (don't rinse) and place in a medium saucepan with 1 cup of water. Bring to a boil, then reduce the heat to low and simmer, covered, for 15 minutes or until the millet has absorbed all the water. Remove from the heat and set aside.

3. At the same time, put the lentils in a medium saucepan with 2 cups of water and also bring to the boil. Reduce the heat to low and simmer, covered, for 15 minutes or until the lentils are tender. Drain and set aside.

4. Place the chickpeas in the bowl of a food processor and pulse a couple of times to break them up. Remove to a large mixing bowl and add the pumpkin puree, beans, lentils and millet.

5. Wipe down the food processor and add the rolled oats. Pulse them a couple of times to break them up into a very rough meal. Add to the mixing bowl.

6. Heat the olive oil in a medium frying pan over medium-high heat. Add the onion and stir for 5 minutes or until softened. Add the garlic, semi sun-dried tomatoes and spices and stir for 1 minute. Add to the mixing bowl along with the mustard, coconut flour, basil, egg and a couple of good grinds of salt and pepper. Use your hands to mix everything together as much as possible.

7. Scoop out heaped ⅓ cup-sized amounts of the mix and form into patties.

8. Heat a tablespoon of oil in a large non-stick frying pan. Cook the patties for 6 minutes, then gently flip and cook for another 6 minutes or until cooked through. Serve warm.

SWEET POTATO PIES

INGREDIENTS

1 tbsp olive oil

1 small onion, finely chopped

2 garlic cloves, crushed

2 tsps curry powder

1 tsp garam masala

1 tsp ground oregano

½ tsp ground cumin

250g (9oz) mushrooms, sliced

2 tsps GF Worcestershire sauce

1 cup (200g, 7oz) cooked brown lentils

Salt and pepper

500g (1lb 2oz) sweet potato, peeled and diced

1 large egg, lightly beaten

¼ cup (60ml, 2fl oz) milk

1 tbsp butter

METHOD

1. Preheat the oven to 180°C (350°F, Gas Mark 4).

2. Heat the oil in a large frying pan over medium-high heat. Add the onion and fry for 5 minutes until softened and browned. Add the garlic and fry for a further minute. Add the curry powder, masala, oregano, cumin and mushrooms and stir for 3 more minutes. Stir in the Worcestershire sauce, then remove from heat, stir in the lentils, season to taste and set aside.

3. Steam the sweet potato for at least 15 minutes or until tender. Whisk the egg and milk together then add to the potato and mash through with the butter. Season to taste.

4. Spread the mushroom mix in the bottom of a baking dish, then spread the sweet potato over the top.

5. Bake for 30 minutes until the topping is slightly browned. Serve hot.

SWEET POTATO FRIES

INGREDIENTS

800g (1¾ lb) sweet potatoes, peeled

Olive oil cooking spray

1 egg white

1 tbsp chickpea flour

Pinch of salt

½ tsp GF garlic powder

¼ tsp cayenne pepper

½ tsp sweet paprika

½ tsp GF onion powder

1 tbsp rosemary leaves, roughly chopped.

Pepper, to taste

METHOD

1. Preheat the oven to 200°C (400°F, Gas Mark 6) and line a large flat baking tray with baking paper sprayed with olive oil.

2. Cut the sweet potatoes into sticks 8cm (3in) long and 1cm (½ in) thick.

3. Place in a large bowl with the rest of the ingredients. Toss everything together until the chips are well coated.

4. Arrange them in an even layer on the baking tray.

5. Bake for 20 minutes, then turn them over and bake for 20 more minutes until cooked through.

MOUSSAKA

INGREDIENTS

Meat sauce

1 tsp olive oil

1 onion, finely chopped

2 garlic cloves, crushed

500g (1lb 2oz) lamb mince

3 tbsps tomato paste

1 x 400g (14oz) can diced tomatoes

⅔ cup (150ml, 5fl oz) vegetable stock

2 tbsps basil, shredded

1 tbsp oregano, chopped

1 tbsp fresh thyme, chopped

¼ tsp allspice

1 tsp pure maple syrup

Salt and pepper

Olive oil cooking spray

3 large eggplants, cut into 1cm (½ in) slices

White sauce

2 tbsps butter

3 tbsps arrowroot flour

1 cup (250ml, 8fl oz) milk

1 cup (250ml, 8fl oz) GF vegetable stock

Pinch of nutmeg

200g (7oz) mozzarella

2 small eggs, lightly beaten

Fresh basil, to garnish

METHOD

1. Preheat the oven to 180°C (350°F, Gas Mark 4) and lightly grease a large deep baking dish.

2. To make the meat sauce, heat the oil in a large, deep-sided frying pan over medium-high heat. Add the onion and fry for 5 minutes until softened, then add the garlic and cook for 1 minute.

3. Add the mince and cook for 5 minutes until browned. Stir through the tomato paste for 2 minutes then pour in the tomatoes, stock, fresh herbs, allspice and maple syrup.

4. Bring to a boil, then reduce heat to low and simmer for 20 minutes or until the sauce has thickened. (For a richer sauce, cover and simmer for up to 3 hours, adding more stock as needed.)

5. Heat a large frying pan over medium-high heat and spray with oil. Cook the eggplant slices for 2 minutes on each side until lightly browned. Let cool on a wire rack.

6. To make the white sauce, melt the butter in a medium saucepan over medium-high heat.

7. Stir in the arrowroot flour for 1 minute. It will thicken considerably. Slowly add the milk, stirring the whole time to avoid lumps while the sauce thickens. Add the vegetable stock and nutmeg and bring to a boil, reduce heat and stir for 3 minutes until reduced to a thick sauce. Stir through half the cheese and eggs and season to taste.

8. Place eggplant slices in a layer on the bottom of the baking dish. Top with a third of the sauce and repeat until the eggplant and sauce are gone. Spread the white sauce over and sprinkle the remaining cheese on top.

9. Bake for 35 minutes or until the top is bubbling and golden.

10. Serve garnished with fresh basil leaves.

KALE AND SWEET POTATO STEW

INGREDIENTS

2 tbsps coconut oil

500g (1lb 2oz) chicken breast, cut into 1½ cm (¾ in) cubes

2 garlic cloves, crushed

2 tsps cumin

1 tsp sweet paprika

¼ tsp crushed chilli flakes

Pinch of turmeric

2 medium sweet potatoes, peeled and cut into 1½ cm (¾ in) cubes

2 medium tomatoes, roughly chopped

¼ cup (60g, 2oz) tomato passata

¼ cup (60ml, 2fl oz) coconut milk

1½ cups (375ml, 13fl oz) GF chicken stock

4 cups (550g, 1¼ lb) packed kale, stems removed, roughly chopped

Salt and pepper

METHOD

1. Heat the oil in a large, deep-sided frying pan over medium-high heat. Add the chicken and garlic, cumin, paprika, chilli flakes and turmeric and fry for 5 minutes until the chicken is mostly cooked through.

2. Add the sweet potatoes and fry for 2 minutes, then add in the tomatoes and tomato paste and stir for 2 minutes more.

3. Pour in the coconut milk and stock and bring to a boil. Reduce the heat to low and simmer, covered, for 15 minutes.

4. Add the kale and stir through. Cover again and cook for 5 minutes or until the kale has just wilted.

5. Season to taste with a couple of good grinds of salt and pepper and serve.

FRIED FLAKE WITH ASIAN SLAW

METHOD

1. To make the slaw, toss together the capsicum, cabbage, radishes and carrot. Whisk together all the other ingredients, season to taste and pour over the slaw. Set aside.

2. To cook the flake, whisk the chickpea flour in a small bowl with the garlic powder, cayenne, paprika, onion powder, a pinch of salt and a couple of good grinds of pepper. Spread out in a shallow dish and gently place each fillet in it to lightly coat both sides.

3. Heat a non-stick frying pan over medium-high heat. Heat the oil and butter together and fry the garlic for about 30 seconds. Add the flake and cook for 3 minutes each side or until cooked through.

4. Serve the fish with roast potatoes and slaw.

INGREDIENTS

Slaw

2 green capsicums, julienned

1 cup (100g, 3½ oz) red cabbage, finely shredded

2 radishes, julienned

1 small carrot, julienned

3 tbsps lime juice

1 tsp garlic, minced

2 tsps fresh ginger, minced

½ tsp ground chilli powder

1 tbsp GF tamari

1 tbsp rice wine vinegar

1 tbsp honey

1 tbsp sesame oil

2 tbsps olive oil

2 tbsps peanuts, chopped

Flake

1 tbsp chickpea flour

½ tsp GF garlic powder

¼ tsp cayenne pepper

½ tsp sweet paprika

½ tsp GF onion powder

Salt and pepper

800g (1 ¾ lb) flake fillets

2 tbsps olive oil

2 tbsps unsalted butter

1 garlic clove, crushed

2 tbsps lemon juice

PORK SCHNITZEL

INGREDIENTS

2 cups (30g, 1oz) puffed rice cereal

1 tsp sweet paprika

1 tsp gluten-free onion powder

1 tsp dried mixed herbs

1 tsp ground fennel

Salt and pepper

2 medium eggs

¼ cup (25g, 1oz) chickpea flour

4 pork schnitzel steaks

Canola or vegetable oil, for frying

Parsley sprigs, to garnish

8 lemon wedges, to serve

METHOD

1. Place the rice cereal in a food processor along with rest of the herbs and spices and a couple of good grinds of salt and pepper.

2. Process until the mixture resembles small breadcrumbs. Transfer the mix to a large shallow plate.

3. Lightly whisk the eggs together and place in a separate shallow bowl.

4. Place the chickpea flour in another shallow plate.

5. Sit the plates in the following order: flour; egg; rice crumbs and another large flat plate on the end.

6. Use a meat mallet to flatten the schnitzels to 5mm (¼ in) thickness.

7. Lightly coat each schnitzel in the flour, then dredge in the egg, shaking off any excess. Coat in the crumbs, pressing them onto the fillet to form a thick, even coating and then place on the plate.

8. Cover and let them rest in the refrigerator for 20 minutes.

9. Heat enough oil in a deep-sided frying pan to come around 5mm (¼ in) up the sides over high heat.

10. Fry the schnitzels two at a time for around 4 minutes each side or until golden brown. Drain them on paper towels.

11. Serve the schnitzels hot, garnished with parsley and lemon wedges on the side.

ROAST CHICKEN AND VEGETABLES

INGREDIENTS

2.4kg (5lb 4oz) whole chicken

⅓ cup (80ml, 3fl oz) olive oil

2 tbsps salt

2 large rosemary sprigs, 1 sprig stripped of leaves

2 tsps GF tamari sauce

8 medium potatoes, washed and cut into wedges

4 large carrots, halved and cut into thick slices

2 small lemons, halved

METHOD

1. Preheat the oven to 220°C (425°F, Gas Mark 7). Pat dry the chicken with paper towels. Tie the legs together with kitchen string.

2. Rub half the oil into the chicken, along with half the salt and the rosemary leaves from the stripped sprig. Then lightly rub the tamari sauce over the chicken as well.

3. Toss the vegetables and lemon with the rest of the oil and salt.

4. Place the chicken in a roasting pan, breast side up and arrange the potatoes, carrots and lemon around it. Place the spare sprig of rosemary in the dish.

5. Roast for 1 hour.

6. Remove the chicken from the pan and set aside, covered.

7. Move the pan with the vegetables to the top third of the oven and roast the vegetables for a further 10 minutes. Serve hot.

SWEET CHILLI CHICKEN AND CHIPS

INGREDIENTS

Chips

Olive oil cooking spray

800g (1¾ lb) sweet potato, peeled

1 egg white

1 tbsp chickpea flour

Pinch of salt

½ tsp GF garlic powder

¼ tsp cayenne pepper

½ tsp sweet paprika

½ tsp GF onion powder

1 tbsp rosemary leaves, roughly chopped

Pepper, to taste

Sweet chilli chicken

3 tbsps olive oil

Salt and pepper

1kg (2lb) chicken drumsticks, skin on

4 tbsps butter

2 garlic cloves, crushed

⅔ cup (160ml, 5fl oz) GF sweet chilli sauce

½ tsp cayenne pepper

1 tsp paprika

3 tbsps pure maple syrup

METHOD

1. To make the chips, preheat the oven to 200°C (400°F, Gas Mark 6) and line a large flat baking tray with baking paper sprayed with olive oil. Cut the sweet potato into wedges of desired shape. Place the wedges in a large bowl with the rest of the ingredients and toss until they are well coated. Arrange in an even layer on the baking tray. Bake for 20 minutes, then turn them over and bake for another 20 minutes until cooked.

2. To make the chicken, heat the oil in a large deep-sided frying pan over medium-high heat. Lightly season the drumsticks then fry in batches for about 10 minutes, until cooked through and skin is golden brown. Drain on paper towels while you cook the rest of the drumsticks.

3. Place the rest of the ingredients in a small saucepan over medium heat and stir until bubbling. Reduce heat and cook for another 5 minutes. Remove from the heat.

4. When all of the drumsticks cooked, return them to the frying pan and drizzle half the sauce over the top. Stir until coated in the sauce.

5. Serve with the chips and the rest of the sauce on the side.

SHEPHERD'S PIE

INGREDIENTS

6 medium potatoes, peeled and cut into 2cm (1in) cubes

1 garlic clove, peeled

Salt and pepper

½ cup (125ml, 4fl oz) milk

½ cup (60g, 2oz) tasty cheese, grated

2 tbsps butter

2 tbsps creme fraiche

1 tbsp olive oil

1 small onion, finely chopped

2 small carrots, finely chopped

1 small celery stalk, finely chopped

700g (1½ lb) minced beef

2 tbsps mixed herbs

1 cup (170g, 6oz) fresh or frozen peas

1 cup (250ml, 8fl oz) GF mushroom stock

1 tbsp red wine vinegar

½ tbsp GF Worcestershire sauce

1 tbsp tomato paste

2 tbsps chickpea flour

METHOD

1. Preheat the oven to 190°C (375°F, Gas Mark 5).

2. Boil the potatoes with the garlic clove and a dash of salt for about 14 minutes until soft and tender.

3. Drain the potatoes, then mash them together with the milk, cheese, butter and creme fraiche. Season to taste and set aside.

4. Heat the oil in a large frying pan over medium-high heat. Add the onion and fry for 5 minutes until softened and browned. Add the carrots and celery and fry for a further 2 minutes. Add the beef and herbs and fry for 8 minutes until the beef is browned, using your wooden spoon to break up the beef.

5. Add the peas, stock, vinegar, Worcestershire sauce, tomato paste and chickpea flour and stir to mix through thoroughly until almost simmering. The liquid should be a thick gravy. If it's too thin, stir 1 teaspoon of chickpea flour together with 1 tablespoon of water then stir it into the beef mixture. Season to taste.

6. Pour the beef mixture into a large casserole dish. Spread the mashed potato over the top and use the back of a spoon or spatula to form little spikes on top.

7. Bake for 30 minutes until browned on top. Let it cool for 10 minutes before serving.

CHICKPEA CHICKEN CURRY

INGREDIENTS

1 tbsp sesame oil

1 small onion, finely chopped

2 garlic cloves, crushed

800g (1¾ lb) chicken breasts, skin removed, cut into bite-size chunks

2 tbsps Thai red curry paste

1 x 400ml (14fl oz) can coconut cream

¼ cup (60ml, 2fl oz) GF chicken stock

1 x 400g (14oz) can chickpeas, rinsed and drained

½ tbsp arrowroot flour

¼ cup (10g, ¼ oz) fresh parsley, roughly chopped

METHOD

1. Heat the oil in a deep frying pan over medium-high heat. Add the onion and fry for 5 minutes until softened and browned. Add the garlic and fry for a further minute.

2. Add the chicken and fry for 6 minutes, until cooked through.

3. Stir the curry paste through to coat the chicken for 2 minutes.

4. Pour in the coconut cream, chicken stock and chickpeas. Stir to combine. Bring to a boil, reduce the heat to low and simmer, covered, for 15 minutes.

5. Stir the arrowroot with about 2 tablespoons of water, then stir into the curry until the sauce thickens. Simmer for another 2 minutes.

6. Let the curry cool for 5 minutes.

7. Serve garnished with chopped parsley.

CAULIFLOWER RICE

INGREDIENTS

1 large head cauliflower, trimmed and cut into florets

1 tbsp coconut oil

1 tbsp fresh ginger, minced

1 tsp GF onion powder

1 tsp GF garlic powder

3 tbsps desiccated coconut

2 tbsps fresh mint, roughly chopped

Salt and pepper

METHOD

1. Place the cauliflower florets into a food processor and pulse until the cauliflower resembles rice.

2. Heat the coconut oil in a large, deep-sided frying pan over medium-high heat. Add the ginger, onion powder and garlic powder and stir for one minute.

3. Add the cauliflower and coconut and cook for 18 minutes until the cauliflower is cooked through and tender.

4. Stir through the mint, season to taste and serve.

BEEF GOULASH

INGREDIENTS

2 tbsps chickpea flour

1 tsp salt

1 tsp pepper

1kg (2lb) trimmed beef cheek, cut into 2½ cm (1in) cubes

3 tbsps butter

1 medium onion, finely chopped

2 garlic cloves, minced

¼ cup (30g, 1oz) sweet paprika

2 tsps caraway seeds

3 cups (750ml, 24fl oz) GF beef stock

½ cup (115g, 4oz) tomato passata

1 tbsp red wine vinegar

2 tbsps sour cream, room temperature

Salt and pepper

¼ cup (10g, ¼ oz) fresh parsley, roughly chopped

METHOD

1. Preheat the oven to 140°C (280°F, Gas Mark 1).

2. Stir together the chickpea flour, salt and pepper and place in a large mixing bowl. Pat the beef dry with paper towels then toss to coat in the flour.

3. Heat the butter in a large ovenproof dish over medium-high heat. Add the onion and fry for 5 minutes until softened and browned. Add the garlic and fry for a further minute. Reduce the heat to low and cook, covered for another 5 minutes.

4. Stir the paprika and caraway seeds into the pan for 1 minute. Turn the heat back up to medium high and add the beef in batches and fry for 5 minutes in the onions until browned. Remove the cooked beef to a separate bowl and set aside.

5. Pour ½ cup of stock into the pan and scrape off anything stuck to the bottom of the pan while it simmers. Stir in the passata and vinegar and cook for 2 minutes.

6. Return the beef to the pan and pour the rest of the stock over the top. Heat until nearly boiling then place the dish in the oven, covered.

7. Cook for 4 hours, until the beef is tender.

8. Stir in the sour cream, season to taste and serve, garnished with parsley.

BEEF MADRAS

INGREDIENTS

1 x 400g (14oz) can tinned tomatoes

2 tbsps coconut oil

1 small onion, finely diced

2 garlic cloves, crushed

800g (1¾ lb) chuck beef, cut into 3cm (1in) chunks

2 tbsps fresh ginger, minced

1 tbsp ground coriander

1 tsp ground cumin

1 tsp ground turmeric

½ tsp ground cardamom

¼ tsp crushed chilli flakes

1 tbsp tomato paste

2 cups (500ml, 1pt) GF beef stock

Salt and pepper

Parsley, to garnish

METHOD

1. Place the tinned tomatoes in a blender or use a stick blender to blend them to a rough puree. Set aside.

2. Heat the oil in a large, deep-sided frying pan with a tight-fitting lid over medium-high heat. Add the onion and fry for 5 minutes until softened and browned. Add the garlic and fry for a further minute.

3. Add the beef in batches and fry for 5 minutes until browned. Remove the cooked beef to a separate bowl and set aside.

4. Add the ginger and spices and fry for 1 minute until fragrant.

5. Stir in the tomato paste. Add the blended tomatoes and beef stock and bring to a boil. Return the beef to the pan and reduce the heat to low. Simmer, covered for 40 minutes. Remove the lid and simmer for 30 minutes until the beef is tender and the gravy is thick.

6. Season beef to taste, garnish with parsley and serve with rice.

ORANGE ROASTED CHICKEN

INGREDIENTS

8 mixed pieces of
chicken, skin on

Salt and pepper

1 tbsp olive oil

1 tbsp butter

6 large garlic cloves,
peeled

1 tbsp pure maple syrup

2 tsps ground cumin

½ tsp chilli flakes

½ cup (125ml, 4fl oz)
orange juice

1½ cups (375ml, 13fl oz)
GF chicken stock

2 large oranges,
sliced, pips removed

2 small red onions,
cut into thick wedges

5 sprigs of thyme

1 sprig fresh rosemary

Rosemary leaves,
to garnish

METHOD

1. Preheat the oven to 190°C (375°F, Gas Mark 5).

2. Pat dry the chicken pieces with paper towels and lightly season
    them.

3. Heat the oil in heatproof and ovenproof Dutch oven over medium-
    high heat. Fry the chicken pieces on each side for 3 minutes until
    slightly browned. Remove from the dish and set aside.

4. Stir in the butter, cloves of garlic, maple syrup, cumin and chilli and
    cook for 1 minute. Add the orange juice and scrape off anything
    sticking to the bottom. Add the stock and bring to a simmer for 3
    minutes.

5. Remove the dish from the heat. Arrange the orange slices in a layer
    on the bottom of the pan. Place the chicken pieces, skin side up, on
    top and scatter the onion wedges, thyme and rosemary over the top.

6. Bake for 60 minutes, covered. Remove the lid and cook for 20
    minutes more to crisp up the skin.

7. Serve hot garnished with rosemary leaves.

PEPPERY PORK CHOPS AND COLESLAW

INGREDIENTS

2 tbsps pure maple syrup

1 tbsp canola oil

1 tbsp apple cider vinegar

1 tsp ground cumin

½ tsp crushed chilli flakes

½ tsp pepper

Pinch of salt

4 pork chops on the bone

Coleslaw

3 cups (300g, 10oz) white cabbage, finely shredded

1½ cups (150g, 5oz) red cabbage, finely shredded

1 cup (50g, 2oz) carrot, coarsely grated

1 large green apple, peeled, cored and grated

1 tbsp olive oil

1 tbsp apple cider vinegar

Salt and pepper

METHOD

1. To make the coleslaw toss all the coleslaw ingredients together in a large mixing bowl along with a couple of good grinds of salt and pepper. Set aside.

2. Whisk together the maple syrup, oil, vinegar, cumin, chilli, pepper and salt in a small mixing bowl.

3. Pat dry the pork chops with paper towels and coat in the pepper mixture.

4. Let the chops sit for at least 30 minutes, covered with plastic wrap.

5. Heat a large frying pan over medium-high heat.

6. Fry the chops for 4 minutes on each side, only turning once. Don't overcrowd the pan or the chops won't brown.

7. Let them sit for 3 minutes before serving.

8. Give them another couple of grinds of pepper and serve with a side of the coleslaw.

POTATO CHEESE PANCAKES

INGREDIENTS

Dipping sauce

1 cup (250ml, 8fl oz) Greek yoghurt

¼ cup (35g, 1¼ oz) cucumber, grated

2 tbsps fresh parsley, finely chopped

Pinch of salt and pepper

Pancakes

3 cups (975g, 2lb 2oz) mashed potatoes

¾ cup (90g, 3oz) tasty cheese, grated

2 tbsps spring onions, finely chopped

1 large egg, lightly beaten

3 tbsps plus ½ cup (45g, 1½ oz) chickpea flour

2 tsps sweet paprika

1 tsp GF onion powder

Salt and pepper

Canola or vegetable oil, for frying

Salt and paprika, for dusting

METHOD

1. To make the dipping sauce, mix together all the ingredients in a mixing bowl. Season further to taste, then set aside.

2. Place the mashed potatoes, cheese, spring onion, egg, the 3 tablespoons of chickpea flour, paprika, onion powder and a couple of good grinds of salt and pepper in a large bowl. Use your hands to mix everything together until thoroughly combined.

3. Scoop out ¼ cup portions of potato mix and flatten into circles around 1cm (½ in) thick.

4. Lightly season the ½ cup of chickpea flour and lightly dredge each pancake in the flour, shaking off any excess.

5. Add 4 tablespoons of oil in a large frying pan over medium-high heat.

6. Fry the pancakes in small batches for 4 minutes on each side until browned and crispy. Transfer to a serving plate and sprinkle over a pinch of salt and paprika. Serving with dipping sauce on the side.

CUCUMBER AND DILL SALAD

INGREDIENTS

¼ cup (60ml, 2fl oz) Greek yoghurt

¼ cup (60ml, 2fl oz) creme fraiche

3 tbsps fresh dill, finely chopped

1 tbsp olive oil

1 tbsp fresh lime juice

Salt and pepper

6 cups (900g, 2lb) Lebanese cucumbers, halved and thinly sliced

1 small red onion, cut into 8 wedges, then thinly sliced

METHOD

1. Add the yoghurt, creme fraiche, dill, olive oil, lime juice and a couple of good grinds of salt and pepper to a small mixing bowl and whisk together.

2. Season to taste.

3. Add the cucumbers and onion and toss to combine.

4. Serve garnished with extra dill.

HERB SPICED PORK TENDERLOIN

INGREDIENTS

2 firm ripe pears

1 tbsp olive oil

3 large garlic cloves, chopped

1 tbsp Dijon mustard

2 tbsps pure maple syrup

2 tsps orange zest, finely grated

2 tsps ground oregano

1 tsp ground fennel

6 sprigs thyme

Salt and pepper

600g (1lb 5oz) pork tenderloin roast

METHOD

1. Preheat the oven to 200°C (400°F, Gas Mark 6) and lightly grease a roasting tin.

2. Halve and core the pears. Then cut a 5mm (¼ in) thick slice off the rounded top of each half. Then sit them with the larger cut part on the bottom of the roasting dish, so you can rest the roast on them.

3. In a small mixing bowl, mix together the oil, garlic, mustard, maple syrup, orange zest, oregano, fennel and leaves from 1 sprig of thyme as well as a couple of good grinds of salt and pepper.

4. Rub into the pork and place the fillet on top of the pears in the dish. Arrange the thyme sprigs on top. Cover with foil and let it sit in the refrigerator for 30 minutes.

5. Bake the roast in the oven for 20 minutes. Remove the foil, and brush any juices in the bottom of the pan over the roast.

6. Increase the oven to 230°C (450°F, Gas Mark 8), return the roast to the oven, uncovered, for 10 minutes.

7. Remove and let it sit, covered, for at least 10 minutes before carving.

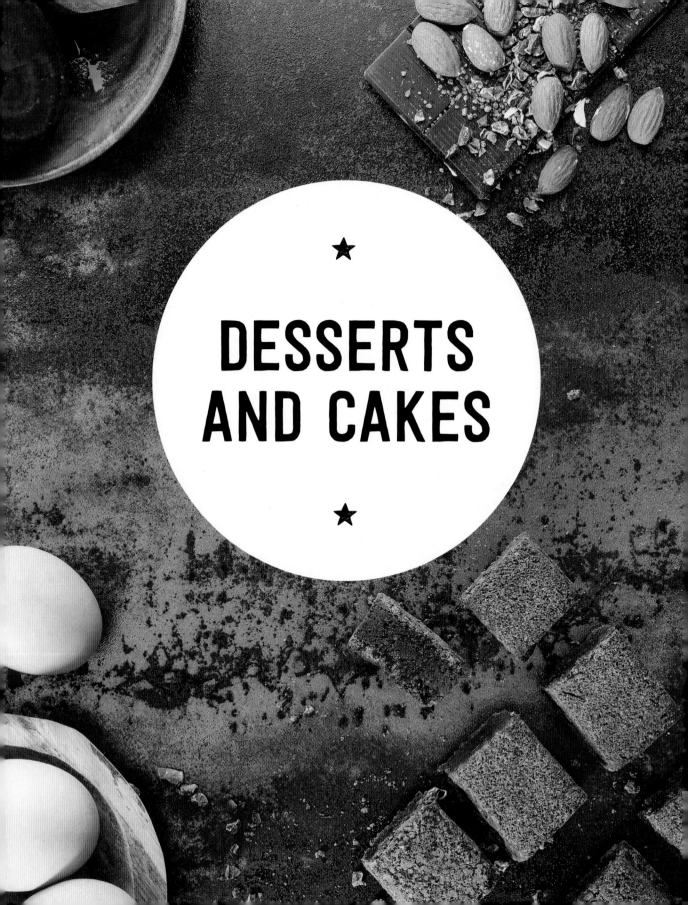

DESSERTS AND CAKES

ALMOND AND BUTTERCREAM LAYER CAKE

INGREDIENTS

Topping

1 tsp almond meal

5 tbsps caster sugar

½ tsp ground cinnamon

1 tbsp unsalted butter, room temperature

Cake

2½ cups (310g, 10oz) GF plain flour

1 tsp xanthan gum

¼ cup (30g, 1oz) plus 2 tbsps arrowroot flour

½ tsp GF bicarbonate of soda

2¼ tsps GF baking powder

½ tsp salt

140g (5oz) unsalted butter, room temperature

1¼ cups (300g, 10oz) caster sugar

2 tsps vanilla extract

3 tsps almond extract

4 large egg whites, room temperature

1 large egg, room temperature

1⅓ cups (330ml, 11fl oz) milk, room temperature

2 cups (450g, 1lb) buttercream frosting (see recipe page 220)

METHOD

1. To make the topping, add all the ingredients into a medium mixing bowl. Press together small amounts of mixture with your fingertips until it resembles coarse sand. Set aside.

2. To make the cake, preheat the oven to 180°C (350°F, Gas Mark 4) and line a 21cm (8in) square deep cake tin with baking paper.

3. Sift together the flours, xantham gum, arrowroot, bicarb, baking powder and salt in a mixing bowl and make a well in the centre.

4. In a large mixing bowl, beat the butter and sugar together until it resembles whipped cream. Add the vanilla and almond extract and mix through.

5. In a separate bowl, whisk the egg whites, egg and milk until light and fluffy.

6. Add the milk mixture and the flour mixture in thirds to the butter mixture, ensuring each portion is just mixed through before adding the next. Beat for a minute or two extra to ensure a thick smooth cake batter.

7. Pour the cake mix into the tin and bake for 40 minutes or until a skewer inserted into the middle comes out clean. Remove from the oven and cool in the tin for 15 minutes before turning out onto a wire rack to cool completely.

8. Slice off the top third of the cake. Spread half of the softened buttercream frosting over the bottom part of the cake and sit the sliced-off section on top of the frosting. Frost the top and sides of the cake with the rest of the buttercream and then press the topping in an even layer over the frosting.

PALEO PUMPKIN BROWNIES

INGREDIENTS

¼ cup (20g, ¾ oz) hazelnut meal

¼ cup (65g, 2oz) almond butter

¾ cup (170g, 6oz) pumpkin puree (see recipe page 17)

1 very ripe large banana

¼ cup (80g, 3oz) agave extract

1 tsp vanilla extract

60g (2oz) butter, melted

1 tbsp coconut flour

1 tsp allspice

1 tsp cinnamon

Pinch of ground cloves

1 tsp GF bicarbonate of soda

Pinch of salt

Topping

1 cup (325g, 11oz) GF apricot jam

1 cup (125g, 4oz) chopped hazelnuts

METHOD

1. Preheat the oven to 180°C (350°F, Gas Mark 4) and line a 20cm (8in) square slice tin with greased baking paper.

2. Whisk together the hazelnut meal, almond butter, pumpkin, banana, agave syrup and vanilla in a mixing bowl until thoroughly combined.

3. Mix through the rest of the ingredients

4. Pour the brownie mixture into the slice tin in a smooth even layer.

5. Bake for 30 minutes or until a skewer inserted into the middle comes out clean.

6. Let cool for 15 minutes, then spread with apricot jam. Cut into roughly 4cm (1½ in) squares and top each with a couple of chopped hazelnuts.

AMARANTH HONEY CAKE

INGREDIENTS

2 medium eggs,
room temperature,
lightly beaten

½ cup (180g, 6oz)
honey

½ cup (125ml, 4fl oz)
espresso coffee,
cooled

½ cup (110g, 4oz)
caster sugar

¼ cup (60ml, 2fl oz)
vegetable oil

¾ cup (95g, 3oz)
brown rice flour

²/₃ cup (75g, 3oz)
tapioca flour

⅓ cup (35g, 1¼ oz)
amaranth flour

1½ tsps xanthan gum

1½ tsps GF baking
powder

½ tsp GF bicarbonate
of soda

¼ tsp cardamom

¼ tsp allspice

Pinch of cinnamon

1 tbsp pure icing sugar,
for dusting

¼ cup (30g, 1oz)
walnuts, to garnish

METHOD

1. Preheat the oven to 160°C (325°F, Gas Mark 3) and line a 28 x 13cm (11 x 5in) loaf tin with greased baking paper.

2. Mix together the eggs, honey, coffee, sugar and oil in a large bowl.

3. Sift together the rest of the cake ingredients into a large mixing bowl and make a well in the centre.

4. Pour in the wet ingredients and whisk through until everything is thoroughly incorporated and the mixture is smooth.

5. Pour into the tin and bake for 45 minutes or until a skewer inserted into the middle comes out clean.

6. Let cool in the tin for 5 minutes before turning out onto a wire rack to cool to room temperature.

7. Dust with icing sugar and decorate with walnuts halves.

CORNMEAL CAKE

INGREDIENTS

Cake

½ cup (80g, 3oz) polenta

⅔ cup (160ml, 5fl oz) milk

250g (9oz) butter

¾ cup (195g, 7oz) packed caster sugar

2 tbsps orange zest

2 tbsps lemon zest

3 large eggs, separated, room temperature

1⅓ cups (180g, 6oz) brown rice flour

70g (2½ oz) potato flour

30g (1oz) white rice flour

25g (1oz) tapioca flour

3 tsps GF baking powder

½ cup (60g, 2oz) flaked almonds

Syrup

½ cup (110ml, 4fl fl oz) orange juice

¼ cup (60ml, 2fl oz) lemon juice

2¼ cups (500g, 1lb) white sugar

Fresh berries and mint leaves, to serve

METHOD

1. Preheat the oven to 180°C (350°F, Gas Mark 4) and line a 25cm (10in) round springform cake tin with greased baking paper.

2. Thirty minutes before starting on the batter, mix the polenta and milk together in a bowl and let the polenta absorb some of the milk.

3. Beat the butter, sugar and zests together until the sugar is dissolved and the mixture is light and fluffy.

4. Beat in the egg yolks one at a time, making sure each one is completely mixed through before adding the next.

5. Sift the flours and baking powder together then add alternating thirds into the egg mixture along with the polenta and milk mixture, ensuring each portion is just mixed through before adding the next.

6. Whisk the egg whites until soft peaks form and fold into the rest of the batter.

7. Sprinkle the flaked almonds in an even layer over the bottom of the cake tin.

8. Pour the cake batter into the cake tin and bake for 1 hour or until a skewer inserted into the middle comes out clean.

9. Remove from the oven but keep the cake in the tin.

10. To make the syrup, stir all the syrup ingredients together in a medium saucepan over medium-high heat and bring a boil.

11. Reduce heat to low and simmer for 3 minutes.

12. Remove from the heat. Use a skewer to poke lots of holes in the cake. Drizzle half the syrup over the cake and let it soak in. After 20 minutes, remove the cake from the tin and invert it onto a serving plate and drizzle the rest of the syrup over the top.

13. Serve topped with fresh summer berries and mint leaves.

FRUIT CAKE

INGREDIENTS

1½ cups (180g, 6oz) almond meal

½ cup (80g, 3oz) light brown sugar

1 tsp ground cardamom

1 tsp allspice

Pinch of ground cloves

½ tsp salt

¼ tsp GF bicarbonate of soda

½ tsp GF baking powder

1 cup (125g, 4oz) walnuts, finely chopped

1½ cups (260g, 9oz) Medjool dates, pitted and chopped

1 cup (160g, 6oz) raisins

3 large eggs, lightly beaten, room temperature

¼ cup (80g, 3oz) agave syrup

1 tbsp pure vanilla extract

METHOD

1. Preheat the oven to 150°C (300°F, Gas Mark 2) and line a 22 x 5cm (8½ x 2in) loaf tin with greased baking paper.

2. Stir together the almond meal, sugar, cardamom, allspice, ground cloves, salt, bicarb and baking powder in a large bowl. Stir through the walnuts, dates and raisins.

3. Beat the eggs, agave and vanilla together in another mixing bowl until smooth.

4. Stir the egg mixture into the dry ingredients and stir to combine thoroughly.

5. Pour the cake batter into the loaf tin and smooth the surface.

6. Bake the fruit cake for around 70 minutes or until a skewer inserted into the middle comes out clean.

7. Let cool in the tin for 30 minutes, then remove the cake to a wire rack to cool to room temperature.

8. Will keep in an airtight container for 2 weeks.

CHOC GLAZED DOUGHNUTS

METHOD

1. To toast the walnuts, preheat a small frying pan over medium-high heat. Dry fry the walnuts for about 4 minutes or until they start to brown. Remove them immediately from the pan and set aside.

2. Preheat the oven to 180°C (350°F, Gas Mark 4) and generously oil a doughnut pan with coconut oil. Set aside.

3. In a large mixing bowl sift together the dry ingredients and make a well in the middle. In a separate bowl whisk together the pumpkin puree, agave, coconut oil and milk. Pour the wet ingredients into the dry and mix together until just combined.

4. Spoon the batter into the doughnut pan and bake for 13 minutes or until the dough springs back when lightly pressed. Let the doughnuts cool for 5 minutes in the pan before placing them on a wire rack then let them cool to room temperature before glazing.

5. To make the glaze, place the glaze ingredients in a small heatproof bowl set over a saucepan of simmering water. Gently stir until the chocolate is melted and the glaze is smooth. Dip the doughnuts in the glaze and sprinkle them with the walnuts, gently pressing them into the glaze. Let them sit for at least 15 minutes. Enjoy!

INGREDIENTS

1 cup (125g, 4oz) walnuts, chopped

Doughnuts

1⅓ cups (180g, 6oz) brown rice flour

70g (2½ oz) potato flour

30g (1oz) white rice flour

25g (1oz) tapioca flour

1 tsp xanthan gum

½ tsp salt

1½ tsps GF baking powder

½ cup (115g, 4oz) pumpkin puree (see recipe page 17)

½ cup (155g, 5oz) agave syrup

2½ tbsps coconut oil, melted

½ cup (125ml, 4fl oz) milk

Glaze

1 cup (155g, 5oz) GF chocolate chips

4 tbsps unsalted butter, chopped

4 tbsps agave syrup

2 tsps water

FRESH FRUIT TART

INGREDIENTS

Shortcrust pastry

1¼ cups (200g, 7oz) rice flour

1⅓ cups (150g, 5oz) tapioca flour

⅔ cup (80g, 30oz) teff flour

⅔ cup (80g, 3oz) brown rice flour

½ cup (80g, 3oz) GF cornflour

¼ cup (35g, 1¼ oz) arrowroot flour

¾ cup (80g, 3oz) almond meal

1½ tsps xanthan gum

2 medium eggs, room temperature

½ cup (120ml, 4fl oz) chilled water

150g (5oz) butter, chilled and grated

120g (4oz) Copha, chilled and grated

Filling

4 ripe pears, halved, cored and thinly sliced

1 tsp allspice

2 tsps orange juice

3 tbsps light brown sugar

2 tbsps butter, chopped

METHOD

1. To make the pastry, sieve the flours into a food processor bowl and add the almond meal and xantham gum. Pulse a few times to mix it all through.

2. Lightly beat the eggs together with 100ml of water and set aside.

3. Add ¼ cup each of the grated butter and Copha to the flours and pulse a few times until the mixture resembles breadcrumbs.

4. Keep adding small amounts of the butter and Copha and pulsing until they're incorporated into the flour mixture.

5. Start the processor running on low speed and slowly drizzle the eggs into the mix until it starts to come together to form a dough.

6. Remove the dough out onto a work surface. Knead for 1 minute then form into a slightly flattened disc. Wrap in plastic wrap and refrigerate for 30 minutes.

7. Preheat the oven to 170°C (340°F, Gas Mark 4) and grease a 26cm (10in) round fluted tart tin with a removable bottom.

8. Roll out the dough into a working surface into a roughly 29cm (12in) circle. Fold in half over the rolling pin and gently lift it into the tart tin. Press the sides into the fluted edge and trim any overhang. Line the pastry with foil and fill with baking beads and bake for 15 minutes. Remove the beads and foil and bake for a further 10 minutes.

9. To make the filling, gently toss the pear slices with the allspice, juice and half the sugar.

10. Arrange the slices in the cooked tart case. Sprinkle over the remaining sugar and scatter the butter over the top.

11. Bake for 35 minutes until the pears are cooked through. Let cool for 10 minutes before removing from the tin. Serve warm.

COCONUT POUND CAKE WITH LIME FROSTING

INGREDIENTS

Lime frosting

225g (9oz) unsalted butter, room temperature

6 cups (930g, 2lb) pure icing sugar

3 tsps lime juice

¼ cup (60ml, 2fl oz) thickened cream

Cake

5 eggs

⅓ cup (80ml, 3fl oz) coconut oil, melted

⅓ cup (105g, 4oz) agave syrup

¼ cup (60ml, 2fl oz) lemon juice

½ cup (60g, 2oz) plus 1 tbsp coconut flour

¼ cup (30g, 1oz) tapioca flour

½ tsp GF bicarbonate of soda

Pinch of salt

2 tbsps lime zest, to decorate

Slices of lime, to decorate

METHOD

1. To make the lime frosting, beat the butter and icing sugar together until the icing sugar is dissolved and the mixture is light and fluffy. Stir in the lime juice and cream then gradually add to the butter mixture and whisk until the buttercream is soft and fluffy. Cover and set aside.

2. Preheat the oven to 180°C (350°F, Gas Mark 4) and line a 23cm (9in) springform cake tin with greased baking paper.

3. In a large mixing bowl, whisk together the eggs, coconut oil, agave syrup and lemon juice. Sift in the coconut flour, tapioca flour, bicarb and salt. Beat until well combined.

4. Pour the cake batter into the cake tin and bake for 35 minutes or until a skewer inserted into the middle comes out clean. Remove from the tin and let cool to room temperature on a wire rack.

5. Cover the top of the cake with the lime frosting. Sprinkle the lime zest over the top and garnish with slices of lime.

LEMON CAKE WITH CASHEW FROSTING

INGREDIENTS

3 tbsps lemon juice

½ cup (125ml, 4fl oz) almond milk

2 tbsps lemon zest

1 cup (220g, 8oz) sugar

½ cup (125ml, 4fl oz) coconut oil

3 eggs, room temperature

½ tsp vanilla extract

2 cups (240g, 8oz) almond meal

1½ tsps GF baking powder

¼ tsp GF bicarbonate of soda

½ tsp salt

Frosting

2¼ cups (280g, 10oz) cashews, soaked for 2 hours

1-2 tbsps lemon juice

2 tbsps coconut oil

⅓ cup (105g, 4oz) pure maple syrup

Water, as needed

2 tsps lemon zest, to garnish

METHOD

1. Preheat oven to 180°C (350°F, Gas Mark 5). Lightly grease 23 x 4cm (9 x 1½ in) round cake tin.

2. Mix together the lemon juice and milk and let sit for 10 minutes. Combine the lemon zest and sugar. Beat together the sugar and coconut oil until thoroughly mixed. Then add the eggs, one at a time until combined. Whisk in the milk and the vanilla extract.

3. In a large mixing bowl, mix the almond meal, baking powder, bicarb and salt and make a well in the centre. Add the wet ingredients to the dry and stir until combined.

4. Pour into the cake tin and bake for 40 minutes, or until a skewer inserted into the middle comes out clean. Let it sit for 15 minutes before turning out onto a wire rack to cool.

5. Place all the frosting ingredients in a high-speed blender and blend until smooth, adding a small amount of water, to hold the frosting together.

6. Once the cake is at room temperature, spread the frosting over the cake and sprinkle lemon zest over the top.

ALMOND AND PISTACHIO SLICE

INGREDIENTS

1 cup (140g, 5oz) unsalted pistachios, shelled

1⅓ cups (160g, 6oz) almond meal

1½ cups (235g, 8oz) pure icing sugar

1 medium egg, room temperature

2 medium egg whites, room temperature

Green food colouring

¾ cup (100g, 3oz) flaked almonds

METHOD

1. Preheat the oven to 170°C (340°F, Gas Mark 4) and line a 20 x 30cm (8 x 12in) slice tin with greased baking paper. Ensure the paper extends out over the sides of the tin by around 4cm (1½ in).

2. Preheat a small frying pan over medium-high heat. Dry fry the pistachios for about 4 minutes or until they start to brown. Remove them immediately from the pan and let them cool for 15 minutes.

3. Place the pistachios in a food processor and pulse until they're ground into a fine meal. Remove to a large mixing bowl and add the almond meal and stir to combine along with the icing sugar.

4. Lightly whisk together the egg and egg whites and stir into the nut mixture. Add one or two drops of food colouring to give it a green tint.

5. Scatter half the flaked almonds over the bottom of the slice tin in an even layer. Drop large spoonfuls of nut mixture over the top then gently smooth the mix out with a spatula in an even layer.

6. Scatter over the rest of the flaked almonds and press down to condense the slice slightly.

7. Bake for 25 minutes or until the almonds start to brown slightly.

8. Remove and let cool for 20 minutes before cutting into squares.

TIRAMISU

INGREDIENTS

2 large eggs, room temperature, separated

⅓ cup (70g, 2½ oz) caster sugar

2½ cups (550ml, 20fl oz) espresso or very strong black coffee, cooled

460g (1lb) mascarpone cheese

400g (14oz) GF lady finger biscuits (can use a GF sponge if you can't find lady finger biscuits), broken into small pieces

150g (5oz) GF dark chocolate, grated

2½ tbsps unsweetened cacao powder

¼ tsp cinnamon

½ cup (50g, 2oz) blueberries, to garnish

Mint leaves, to garnish

METHOD

1. In a medium bowl, whisk the egg yolks and sugar together for 1 minute until the mixture is thick and pale. Add ¼ cup coffee and the mascarpone and whisk until the mixture is smooth.

2. In a separate bowl, whisk the egg whites until soft peaks form. Gently fold the egg white into the mascarpone mixture.

3. Sprinkle the remaining coffee over the biscuits.

4. Layer 1 large dessertspoon of biscuit pieces in the bottom of each of six dessert glasses. Sprinkle about half of the grated chocolate over the layer of biscuit and layer over that around half of the mascarpone mixture. Repeat with the biscuits and mascarpone, then cover the glasses with plastic wrap and refrigerate overnight.

5. When you are ready to serve, place the cacao powder in a small sieve with the cinnamon and dust over the top of the tiramisu.

6. Serve garnished with blueberries and mint leaves.

RASPBERRY PANNA COTTA

INGREDIENTS

Raspberry jelly

2 cups (250g, 8oz) fresh raspberries

2 tsps caster sugar

¼ cup (60ml, 2fl oz) water

4 gold-strength gelatine leaves

Panna cotta

1½ cups (375ml, 13fl oz) cream

½ cup (115g, 4oz) caster sugar

2¼ cups (560ml, 19 fl oz) Greek yoghurt

¾ cup (75g, 3oz) fresh blueberries, to garnish

6 sprigs mint, to garnish

METHOD

1. Heat raspberries in a small saucepan over medium heat for 10 minutes until they disintegrate. Push through a sieve back into the saucepan to remove seeds and any solids. Heat the puree over medium heat and stir in the sugar and enough water to make 130ml of raspberry liquid. Soak 1 gelatine leaf in cold water for 3 minutes. Add the gelatine leaf to the warm liquid; stir until dissolved. Remove from heat and cool for 30 minutes.

2. Soak the remaining gelatine leaves in cold water for 3 minutes. Gently whisk together the cream and sugar in a medium saucepan over medium-high heat and bring slowly to the boil, stirring constantly, until the sugar dissolves. Remove from heat.

3. Squeeze the sheets to remove excess liquid and whisk them into the hot cream until dissolved. Strain the cream through a fine sieve into a large bowl and whisk in the yoghurt.

4. Pour the mixture into six large dessert glasses about two-thirds of the way up. Chill in the refrigerator for at least 3 hours.

5. Pour the jelly on top of the panna cotta in each glass then chill in the refrigerator for 3 more hours. Garnish and serve.

RED VELVET ROULADE

INGREDIENTS

Filling

225g (8oz) cream cheese, room temperature

110g (4oz) GF white cooking chocolate

55g (2oz) unsalted butter, room temperature

½ cup (80g, 3oz) pure icing sugar, sifted

Roulade

½ cup (75g, 2½ oz) brown rice flour

30g (1oz) potato flour

¼ cup (25g, 1oz) coconut flour

2½ tsps GF bicarbonate of soda

Pinch of salt

½ cup (125ml, 4fl oz) milk

1 tsp vanilla extract

1 tsp white vinegar

2 tsps rosewater

230g (8oz) unsalted butter, room temperature

¾ cup (165g, 6oz) caster sugar

1 large egg, room temperature

Red food colouring

2 tbsps pure icing sugar

½ tbsp nigella seeds, to garnish

METHOD

1. To make the filling, beat the cream cheese until smooth and light.

2. Place the white chocolate in a small heatproof bowl set over a saucepan of hot water and stir until melted, then remove from the heat and add to the cream cheese.

3. Beat in the butter until mixed through, then beat in the icing sugar until light and fluffy. Set aside.

4. Preheat the oven to 180°C (350°F, Gas Mark 4) and line a 25 x 30cm (10 x 12in) Swiss roll pan with greased baking paper.

5. Sift together the flours, bicarb and salt and set aside.

6. Mix together the milk, vanilla, vinegar and rosewater and set aside.

7. Beat the butter and sugar together until it resembles whipped cream. Add the egg and completely mix through.

8. Add the flours to the mixture in thirds, alternating with the milk mixture, ensuring each portion is just mixed through before adding the next. Whisk until smooth, then add a couple of drops of red colouring until tinted to a reddish pink.

9. Pour into the tin and bake for 20 minutes or until a skewer inserted into the middle comes out clean.

10. Place a large sheet of baking paper on a wire rack and sprinkle the baking paper with sifted icing sugar. Carefully turn the cake out on top of the prepared baking paper. Remove the top layer of baking paper and allow cake to cool.

11. Spread the filling evenly over the cake. Carefully roll the cake, then wrap tightly in plastic wrap and refrigerate for at least 1 hour. When ready to serve, place the cake roll on a serving platter, sprinkle with nigella seeds and cut into slices.

CHOCOLATE MOLTEN LAVA CAKE

INGREDIENTS

100g (3½ oz) unsalted butter, plus extra to grease

¼ cup (30g, 1oz) cacao powder

100g (3½ oz) dark GF cooking chocolate (70% cocoa solids or higher), chopped

2 large eggs, room temperature

2 large egg yolks, room temperature

²/₃ cup (120g, 4oz) caster sugar

½ tsp vanilla extract

½ cup (70g, 2½ oz) brown rice flour

30g (1oz) potato flour

¼ cup (25g, 1oz) coconut flour

6 small sprigs of mint, to garnish

METHOD

1. Preheat the oven to 180°C (350°F, Gas Mark 4) and liberally grease six small individual pudding ramekins or dariole moulds with butter. Then dust with cacao powder.

2. In a small heatproof bowl set over a saucepan of hot water, slowly melt the chocolate and butter. Remove bowl from heat and stir until smooth – try not to stir too much as it makes the filling less glossy. Let cool for 10 minutes.

3. Beat the eggs, yolks, sugar and vanilla extract together until pale and thickened. Use a whisk or slotted spoon to fold in the melted chocolate. Sift the flours over the mixture and again fold in to combine.

4. Divide the batter between the ramekins and bake for 12 minutes.

5. Carefully loosen the puddings from the moulds so as not to break the cake part. Set them upside down on serving plates. Dust lightly with remaining cacao powder and garnish with sprigs of mint.

RASPBERRIES AND CREAM SUMMER PARFAIT

INGREDIENTS

¼ cup (40g, 1½ oz) chia seeds

1 tsp cacao powder

1 cup (250ml, 8fl oz) coconut milk

¼ tsp vanilla extract

1 cup (125g, 4oz) fresh or thawed frozen raspberries

1½ tbsps agave syrup

½ cup (125ml, 4fl oz) thickened cream

1 tsp caster sugar (optional)

½ cup (125ml, 4fl oz) coconut cream

½ cup (125ml, 4fl oz) Greek yoghurt

Fresh raspberries, to garnish

2 tbsps coconut flakes

Mint leaves, to garnish

METHOD

1. Place chia seeds, cacao powder, coconut milk and vanilla in a sealable jar. Shake vigorously to combine and refrigerate overnight.

2. To make the raspberry layer, Heat the raspberries with 2 tablespoons of water in a small saucepan over medium heat for 10 minutes until they disintegrate. Whisk in the agave syrup and add more if needed. Remove from heat and let cool.

3. Beat the cream until stiff peaks form, add the sugar and coconut cream and beat until soft peaks form. Then add the Greek yoghurt and beat again until soft peaks form.

4. To assemble, spoon a layer of the chia seeds into the bottom of two serving glasses, top with a layer of raspberry, then the coconut cream.

5. Arrange fresh raspberries on the top and sprinkle over some coconut flakes.

6. Garnish with mint leaves.

RUSTIC POLENTA CAKE WITH FRESH BERRIES

INGREDIENTS

225g (8oz) unsalted butter, room temperature

1 cup (225g, 8oz) caster sugar

1 tsp vanilla extract

1¾ cups (225g, 8oz) almond meal

3 large eggs, room temperature

2 tbsps lemon zest

2 tbsps orange zest

¼ cup (60ml, 2fl oz) orange juice, strained

¾ cup (115g, 4oz) polenta

1 tsp GF baking powder

½ tsp salt

½ cup (50g, 2oz) flaked almonds

⅓ cup (50g, 2oz) coconut sugar

1 cup (200g, 7oz) fresh strawberries, to serve

½ cup (50g, 2oz) fresh or frozen cranberries, to serve

METHOD

1. Preheat the oven to 160°C (325°F, Gas Mark 3) and line a 20cm (8in) springform cake tin with greased baking paper.

2. In a large mixing bowl, beat the butter and sugar together until it resembles whipped cream. Add the vanilla and almond meal and fold through.

3. Beat in the eggs one at a time, making sure each one is completely mixed through before adding the next.

4. Add the zests, juice, one third of the polenta, the baking powder and salt and mix through.

5. Add the rest of the polenta in halves, ensuring it's only just mixed through before adding the next portion. Don't overmix the batter, leave the last portion of polenta just mixed through.

6. Bake in the oven for about 80 minutes or until cooked and golden brown and a skewer inserted into the centre comes out clean.

7. Remove from the oven and immediately sprinkle the flaked almonds and coconut sugar over the top. Spray some chilled water over the top, then return the cake to the oven and bake for 10 minutes until the almonds are just starting to brown.

8. Let the cake cool in the tin for 10 minutes before removing to a wire rack.

9. Serve with fresh strawberries and scatter some cranberries over the top.

CARROT CAKE PUDDING

INGREDIENTS

Carrot cake

2 cups (100g, 3½ oz) carrot, finely grated

1 large red apple, peeled, cored and finely grated

½ cup (60g, 2oz) coconut flour

¼ cup (60ml, 2fl oz) butter, melted

¼ cup (80g, 3oz) agave syrup

4 medium eggs, room temperature, lightly beaten

½ tsp GF bicarbonate of soda

¼ tsp salt

½ tsp allspice

¼ tsp ground cloves

Cream

2½ cups (600ml, 21fl oz) cream

1 tbsp caster sugar

1 tsp vanilla extract

1 tsp cinnamon

2 tbsps light brown sugar

METHOD

1. To make the carrot cake, preheat the oven to 180°C (350°F, Gas Mark 4) and line a 20cm (8in) round springform cake tin with greased baking paper.

2. Place all the cake ingredients in the bowl of a food processor and blend until thoroughly mixed through.

3. Pour into the cake tin and bake for 40 minutes or until a skewer inserted into the middle comes out clean. Turn out onto a wire rack.

4. Beat the cream until soft peaks form, then add the sugar, vanilla and cinnamon and beat until stiff peaks form.

5. Break up the cake into small pieces and completely crumble ¼ cup of cake.

6. To assemble, place ¼ cup of cake pieces in the bottom of eight dessert glasses, then top with a large spoonful of cream. Repeat.

7. Mix the ¼ cup crumbled cake with the light brown sugar and sprinkle over the top of each glass. Serve while the cake is still warm.

SERVES 4 ★ PREP 20MIN ★ COOK TIME 1HR 40MIN

CHOCOLATE BEETROOT CAKE

INGREDIENTS

2 medium beetroots, ends trimmed, peeled

2 cups (500ml, 1pt) milk

1 tbsp cream of tartar

1½ cups (330g, 12oz) caster sugar

½ cup (125ml, 4fl oz) melted butter

1 tbsp vanilla extract

2 cups (180g, 6oz) GF oat flour

¾ cup (90g, 3oz) almond meal

½ cup (60g, 2oz) cocoa powder

2 tsps GF bicarbonate of soda

1 tsp GF baking powder

Pinch of salt

1 tbsp icing sugar, for dusting

Mint leaves, to garnish

METHOD

1. Preheat the oven to 200°C (400°F, Gas Mark 6). Wrap the beetroots separately in foil and bake until tender for 60 minutes. Let cool, then peel, roughly chop and puree in a blender or with a stick blender until smooth. You need 1 cup of puree.

2. To make the cake, reduce the oven temp to 180°C (350°F, Gas Mark 4). Line a 22cm springform cake tin with greased baking paper.

3. Whisk together the milk and cream of tartar in a bowl. It will curdle after about 5 minutes, which is what you want. Whisk in the beetroot puree, the caster sugar, melted butter and vanilla. Keep whisking until the mixture is light and foamy for 1 minute.

4. Mix together the rest of the dry ingredients, then beat into the mixture, a third at a time, ensuring each portion is just mixed in before adding the next.

5. Pour the batter into the cake tin and bake for 40 minutes or until a skewer inserted into the middle comes out clean.

6. Very gently turn out to cool on a wire rack. To serve, dust with icing sugar and decorate with mint leaves.

CHERRY PAVLOVA

INGREDIENTS

Cherries in syrup

380g (13oz) fresh cherries, halved and pitted

½ cup (100g, 3½ oz) caster sugar

1 cup (250ml, 8fl oz) red wine

1½ tsps arrowroot flour

1½ tbsps red wine vinegar

¼ tsp vanilla extract

Meringues

4 egg whites, room temperature

1 cup (220g, 8oz) caster sugar

1 tsp cream of tartar

1 tsp vanilla essence

Filling

⅔ cup (150ml, 5fl oz) thickened cream

½ cup (125ml, 4fl oz) creme fraiche

2 tbsps icing sugar

Topping

12 fresh cherries, stems intact

6 sprigs mint, to garnish

METHOD

1. To make the cherries in syrup, place the cherries and sugar in a large saucepan over medium heat.

2. Stir together a tablespoon of the wine with the arrowroot in a small glass and set aside.

3. Pour the remaining wine and the vinegar into the saucepan and bring the mixture to a boil. Reduce the heat to low and simmer, stirring every couple of minutes for 15 minutes until the cherries have softened. Give the arrowroot mixture a quick stir again and then pour into the cherries and stir through. Bring back up to a boil for 3 minutes then remove from heat, stir through the vanilla extract and let cool.

4. To make the meringues, preheat the oven to 150°C (300°F, Gas Mark 2) and line two large baking trays with baking paper.

5. Beat the egg whites until stiff peaks form. Add the sugar in thirds along with the cream of tartar and vanilla. Keep beating until stiff peaks form.

6. Spoon out six small heaped portions of the meringue onto the baking trays. Heap the meringue up on the edges and make a small hollow in the middle.

7. Bake for 25 minutes until they are just browning on the edges. Turn off the oven and let them cool to room temperature inside the oven.

8. Whip the cream until stiff peaks form then add the creme fraiche and sugar and beat until the sugar is dissolved and soft peaks form.

9. Spoon the cream mixture into centres of meringues and top with the cherries in syrup, then garnish with a couple of fresh cherries and sprigs of mint.

CHICKPEA CHOC-CHIP COOKIES

INGREDIENTS

1¼ cups (240g, 8oz) canned chickpeas, rinsed and drained

½ tbsp vanilla extract

⅔ cup (165g, 6oz) GF cashew butter

4 tbsps agave syrup

1¼ tsps GF baking powder

Pinch of salt

⅔ cup (100g, 3oz) GF chocolate chips

METHOD

1. Preheat the oven to 180°C (350°F, Gas Mark 4) and line two large flat baking trays with baking paper.

2. Pat dry the chickpeas and place in the bowl of a food processor. Pulse a few times to break them up.

3. Add the vanilla, cashew butter, agave, baking powder and salt and process until the mixture is smooth.

4. Transfer the cookie dough to a large mixing bowl and stir through the chocolate chips.

5. Roll the mixture into around 12 small balls of dough.

6. Place on the baking trays and flatten slightly. Leave at least 4cm (1½ in) space between the cookies.

7. Bake for 12 minutes until golden.

8. Remove to a wire rack to cool slightly.

GINGER BISCUITS

INGREDIENTS

125g (4oz) butter

¼ cup (90g, 3oz) golden syrup

⅓ cup (115g, 4oz) maple syrup

2½ cups (310g, 10oz) plain GF flour

1½ tbsps ground ginger

1 tbsp fresh ginger, minced

1 tsp GF bicarbonate of soda

1 tsp ground cinnamon

¼ tsp GF baking powder

1 tbsp ground flaxseeds, combined with 3 tbsps water

¼ cup (60ml, 2fl oz) water

METHOD

1. Preheat oven to 180°C (350°F, Gas Mark 4). Line a large flat baking tray with baking paper.

2. Melt the butter together with the golden syrup and maple syrup in a medium saucepan. Remove from heat and set aside.

3. In a large mixing bowl, mix together the flour, gingers, bicarb, cinnamon and baking powder. Make a well in the centre.

4. Mix the flaxseed mixture with butter and syrups and then pour into the mixing bowl. Stir together to form a dough; add the water in small doses if you need it. You may not it all.

5. Roll heaped tablespoons of the dough into small balls and place on the baking tray. Flatten slightly and ensure you leave space between each one as they will spread.

6. Bake for 15 minutes, until golden. Reduce the temperature to 140°C (285°F, Gas Mark 1) and bake the biscuits for a further 25 minutes.

7. Let the biscuits cool for at least 10 minutes before removing them to a wire rack to cool completely.

SERVES 4 ★ PREP 50min (PLUS CHILLING) ★ COOK TIME 1hr 20min

PUMPKIN CREME BRULEE

INGREDIENTS

Pumpkin puree

2 cups (170g, 6oz) butternut pumpkin, peeled and cut into 3cm (1in) chunks

1 tsp cinnamon

1½ tsp allspice

¼ tsp nutmeg

¼ tsp ground cloves

Brulee

1½ cups (375ml, 13fl oz) thickened cream

½ cup (125ml, 4fl oz) milk

¼ tsp vanilla extract

¼ tsp allspice

¼ tsp ground ginger

Pinch of ground cloves

4 egg yolks, room temperature

½ cup (110g, 4oz) caster sugar

⅓ cup (50g, 2oz) light brown sugar, for sprinkling

METHOD

1. To make the pumpkin puree, preheat the oven to 160°C (325°F, Gas Mark 3) and line a large flat baking tray with baking paper. Scatter the pumpkin over the tray in an even layer and bake for 40 minutes or until mushy. Puree the pumpkin in a blender until smooth with the cinnamon, allspice, nutmeg and cloves. You need ¼ cup of puree for this recipe.

2. Reduce the oven to 150°C (300°F, Gas Mark 2)

3. Place the cream, milk, vanilla, allspice, ginger and cloves into a medium saucepan over medium-high heat and bring to a boil. Remove from the heat, cover with a tight-fitting lid and sit for 15 minutes.

4. Whisk together the egg yolks and the caster sugar in a large mixing bowl until smooth and light in colour. Gradually add the cream mixture until completely mixed through. Then whisk in the pumpkin puree. Divide the mixture between four ramekins.

5. Place a tea towel in the bottom of a large deep-sided baking dish and sit the ramekins on top. Fill the dish with enough hot water to come halfway up the sides of the ramekins.

6. Bake for 40 minutes or until the creme brulees are set.

7. Remove them from the oven and let them sit for 1 hour, then place in the refrigerator to chill for at least 2 hours.

8. Just before serving, sprinkle the brown sugar over the top of each creme brulee. Use a kitchen torch to melt the sugar until it forms a slightly browned crispy top.

BREADS
AND
LOAVES

SERVES 4 ★ PREP 40MIN ★ COOK TIME 1HR

VEGETABLE LOAF

INGREDIENTS

2 large zucchinis

1 large carrot

2 small red capsicums

2 large Roma tomatoes

2 small yellow squash

4 large eggs, lightly beaten

⅓ cup (100ml, 3½ fl oz) milk

2 tbsps olive oil

4 tbsps grated Romano cheese

½ tbsp dried basil

Salt and pepper

⅓ cup (50g, 2oz) brown rice flour

25g (1oz) tapioca flour

¼ cup (25g, 1oz) chickpea flour

¾ tsp GF baking powder

¼ cup (5g, ¼ oz) fresh basil leaves, to garnish

METHOD

1. Preheat the oven to 180°C (350°F, Gas Mark 4) and line a large loaf tin with greased baking paper.

2. Use a mandolin to slice the vegetables lengthwise into long thin strips about 2mm (⅛ in) thick.

3. Whisk together the eggs, milk, olive oil, Romano cheese and basil along with a couple of good grinds of salt and pepper.

4. Sift together the flours with the baking powder in a mixing bowl and make a well in the centre. Whisk the egg mixture into the flour until thoroughly incorporated.

5. Pour a third of the mix into the tin. Arrange a third of the vegetables lengthwise along the tin. Pour another third of the egg mixture in the tin. Repeat until you've got a layer of vegetables on top. Drizzle with some extra olive oil.

6. Cover with foil and bake for 40 minutes. Remove the foil and bake for a further 20 minutes or until a skewer inserted into the middle comes out clean.

7. Turn the oven off and let the loaf cool in the oven with door open – this will help pull out a lot of moisture from the vegetables.

8. Before serving, garnish with fresh basil leaves.

SERVES 8 ★ PREP 15MIN (PLUS SOAKING) ★ COOK TIME 1HR 30MIN

BUCKWHEAT BREAD

INGREDIENTS

2 cups (340g, 12oz) raw buckwheat, soaked in water for at least 6 hours, preferably overnight

2 tbsps chia seeds mixed with 2 tbsps warm water

½ cup (125ml, 4fl oz) water

1 tbsp ground flaxseed

1 tbsp olive oil

2 tsps salt

2 tsps GF baking powder

½ cup (60g, 2oz) sunflower seeds, roughly chopped

METHOD

1. Preheat the oven to 180°C (350°F, Gas Mark 4) and grease a 22 x 13cm (10 x 5in) loaf tin with olive oil.

2. Drain and rinse the buckwheat twice.

3. Place all the ingredients, except the sunflower seeds, in a food processor and pulse until you have a smooth mixture.

4. Remove the mixture to a large mixing bowl and stir through the sunflower seeds.

5. Pour the bread mixture into the loaf tin. Bake for 1 hour, then remove the loaf from the tin, place on a wire rack and bake for 30 minutes more.

6. Let the bread cool completely before eating or it may sink.

CORNBREAD WITH FIGS

INGREDIENTS

¾ cup (80g, 3oz) chickpea flour

⅓ cup (40g, 1½ oz) brown rice flour

½ cup (40g, 2oz) coconut flour

½ cup (75g, 2½ oz) fine polenta

2 tsps GF baking powder

½ tsp salt

3 medium eggs, room temperature

½ cup (100g, 3½ oz) caster sugar

½ cup (125ml, 4fl oz) canola oil

⅓ cup (115g, 4oz) honey

1 tsp vanilla extract

1 cup (250ml, 8fl oz) Greek yoghurt

½ cup (75g, 3oz) red apple, peeled, grated

1 cup (150g, 5oz) chopped fresh figs (can use ¾ cup dried figs)

METHOD

1. Preheat the oven to 180°C (350°F, Gas Mark 4) and line a 22 x 13cm (10 x 5in) loaf tin with greased baking paper.

2. Add the flours, polenta, baking powder and salt to a large mixing bowl. Give a stir to mix everything through and make a well in the centre.

3. In a separate mixing bowl, whisk together the eggs, sugar, oil, honey and vanilla. Then stir through the yoghurt and apple until mixed through.

4. Pour the yoghurt mix into the dry ingredients and stir through. Add the figs and fold into the mixture.

5. Pour the batter into the loaf tin and bake for 55 minutes or until a skewer inserted into the middle comes out clean.

6. Let cool for 10 minutes in the tin before turning out onto a wire rack to cool. Serve warm or cold.

SERVES 8 ★ PREP 15MIN (PLUS RESTING) ★ COOK TIME 45MIN

FLAX LOAF

INGREDIENTS

1½ cups (375ml, 13fl oz) plus 1 tbsp warm water

2 tbsps maple syrup

8g (¼ oz) active dry yeast

60g (2oz) ground flaxseeds

¾ cup (120g, 4oz) sorghum flour

½ cup (90g, 3oz) potato flour

½ cup (55g, 2oz) quinoa flour

¼ cup (25g, 1oz) chickpea flour

¼ cup (30g, 1oz) tapioca flour

2½ tsps xanthan gum

1 tsp salt

2 tbsps butter, melted

2 tsps apple cider vinegar

METHOD

1. Grease a 22 x 13cm (10 x 5in) loaf tin with olive oil and dust with extra quinoa flour.

2. Mix 1 cup of the warm water with the maple syrup and the yeast in a small bowl. The yeast will foam slightly. Let it sit for 5 minutes.

3. Add the rest of the water to a stand mixer bowl and stir in 3 tablespoons of the flaxseed. Let it thicken to a gel-like consistency.

4. In a separate mixing bowl, mix together the remaining ground flaxseed, all the flours, the xanthan and salt.

5. Add the butter and vinegar to the thickened flaxseed mixture and stir to combine. Turn the stand mixer to low and slowly add the yeast mix and the flours.

6. Remove the dough to the loaf tin and smooth the top over.

7. Place the dough in a warm, draft-free position and let it prove for around 1 hour or until the top of the loaf is level with the top of the tin.

8. Preheat the oven to 180°C (350°F, Gas Mark 4) about 15 minutes before the 1 hour proving period is up.

9. Bake for 45 minutes or until it comes away from the sides of the tin and sounds hollow when knocked.

10. Carefully remove from the tin and let cool on a wire rack to room temperature before slicing.

MASHED POTATO BREAD

INGREDIENTS

100g (3½ oz) mashed potato

Enough warm water to make up 1 cup (250ml, 8fl oz) when combined with the potato

1 tbsp unsalted butter, room temperature

1½ tbsps agave syrup

½ tsp salt

¾ cup (95g, 3oz) brown rice flour

½ cup (90g, 3oz) potato flour

¼ cup (30g, 1oz) tapioca flour

¼ cup (40g, 1½ oz) white rice flour

4g (¼ oz) instant yeast powder

METHOD

1. Add all the bread ingredients to the bowl of a stand mixer and use the kneading attachment for 7 minutes.

2. Let it sit, covered with a damp tea towel, for 30 minutes to let the dough rise. Knock it back and let it rise again, covered, until nearly doubled in size.

3. Preheat the oven to 180°C (350°F, Gas Mark 4) and grease and lightly dust with brown rice flour a 22 x 13cm (10 x 5in) loaf tin. Form the dough into a loaf shape and place in the tin. Place the loaf, covered, in a warm spot and let rise until just level with the top of the tin.

4. Bake for 30 minutes or until golden brown. Remove from the tin and let it cool to room temperature before slicing.

MULTIGRAIN BREAD

INGREDIENTS

1 cup (125g, 4oz) sunflower seeds

½ cup (75g, 3oz) flaxseed

½ cup (60g, 2oz) hazelnuts, roughly chopped

1½ cups (130g, 4½ oz) GF rolled oats

2 tbsps chia seeds

3 tbsps psyllium husks

1 tsp salt

1½ tbsps agave syrup

3 tbsps unsalted butter, melted

1⅓ cups (350ml, (12fl oz) water

METHOD

1. Oil a loaf tin and set aside.

2. Place the sunflower seeds, flaxseed, hazelnuts, oats, chia seeds, psyllium and salt into a mixing bowl and stir to mix.

3. Whisk together the agave syrup, butter and water in a mixing bowl and tip into the dry ingredients. Mix well to combine.

4. Press the mixture into the loaf tin and smooth the top.

5. Let the bread sit in the tin for at least 4 hours, preferably overnight. The grains and nuts should absorb the water so much that they become a nearly solid mass.

6. Preheat the oven to 180°C (350°F, Gas Mark 4).

7. Bake the loaf for 20 minutes. Remove the bread from the tin then cook it on a rack in the oven for 35 minutes.

8. Let it cool to room temperature before slicing.

CRUNCHY CRISPBREAD

INGREDIENTS

¼ cup (30g, 1oz) pepitas (pumpkin seeds)

¼ cup (30g, 1oz) sunflower seeds

¼ cup (40g, 1½ oz) flaxseed

¼ cup (40g, 1½ oz) hemp seeds

2 tbsps sesame seeds

2 tbsps chia seeds

1 tbsp psyllium husk powder

1¼ cups (300ml, 10fl oz) water

2 tbsps unsalted butter, room temperature

1 tsp ground oregano

1 tsp GF garlic powder

1 tsp salt

METHOD

1. Preheat the oven to 150°C (300°F, Gas Mark 2) and line two large flat baking trays with baking paper.

2. Mix together the seeds and psyllium powder in a bowl and set aside.

3. Boil the water in a large pot. Remove the pot from the heat and stir in the butter until it melts. Pour the seed mixture, oregano, garlic powder and half the salt in and stir until everything is combined. Let it sit for 5 minutes and it should thicken into a jelly-like consistency.

4. Spread the warm mixture out over the pans in a smooth thin layer, about 5mm (¼ in) thick. Sprinkle the remaining salt over the top.

5. Bake for 40 minutes until browned on top. Remove from the oven and use a pizza cutter to cut into desired crispbread squares.

6. Turn the oven temperature down to 60°C (135°F) and bake for 1 hour to dry the squares out until they're crisp and crunchy.

7. Let them cool to room temperature in the oven.

SERVES 6-8 ★ PREP 15MIN (PLUS COOLING) ★ COOK TIME 55MIN

CRISP ALMOND BREAD

INGREDIENTS

4 large eggs, room temperature

½ cup (110g, 4oz) raw sugar

¾ cup (75g, 3oz) coconut flour

¼ cup (30g, 1oz) tapioca flour

½ cup (60g, 2oz) almond meal

METHOD

1. Preheat the oven to 180°C (350°F, Gas Mark 4) and line a thin, long loaf tin with baking paper (place a dab of butter underneath the paper so it stays in place)
2. Separate the eggs and beat the egg whites until stiff peaks form. Slowly stream in the sugar while beating until it's dissolved into the whites.
3. Sift the flours together and stir them through along with the almond meal.
4. Place dollops of the mix along the bottom of the loaf tin and smooth them into one long loaf. The mixture is very sticky so be patient.
5. Bake for 40 minutes, let cool on a wire rack to room temperature before cutting into 1cm (½ in) slices with a sharp serrated knife.
6. Line a large flat baking tray with baking paper and lay the slices out on the tray. Bake for 6 minutes on each side.
7. Let cool to room temperature again on a wire rack or eat them warm.

SERVES 6-8 ★ PREP 30MIN ★ COOK TIME 45MIN

CAULIFLOWER TOMATO LOAF

INGREDIENTS

1 cup (55g, 2oz) semi-sun-dried tomatoes

5 large eggs (separated)

1¼ cups (125g, 4oz) coconut flour

1½ tbsps GF baking powder

1 tsp salt

3 tbsps unsalted butter

3 garlic cloves, crushed

3 cups (975g, 2lb 2oz) cauliflower rice (see recipe page 107)

1 tbsp thyme leaves

½ tbsp rosemary, finely chopped

METHOD

1. Preheat the oven to 180°C (350°F, Gas Mark 4) and line a 22 x 13cm (10 x 5in) loaf tin with baking paper.

2. Place the tomatoes in a blender to create a thick puree.

3. Beat the egg whites until soft peaks form and set aside.

4. Add the tomato puree, coconut flour, baking powder, salt, egg yolks, butter and garlic to a food processor bowl.

5. Place the cauliflower rice in a sieve and press it to squeeze out excess liquid. Add the cauliflower to the processor and mix everything until well combined. Remove the mixture to a large mixing bowl and fold the egg whites through.

6. Transfer the batter into the lined tin and smooth the top with a spoon or spatula. Sprinkle the thyme and rosemary over the top and gently press into the loaf.

7. Bake for about 45 minutes, until the top is browned. Cool completely before removing and slicing.

SERVES 4-6 ★ PREP 10MIN ★ COOK TIME 20MIN
ROSEMARY FOCACCIA

INGREDIENTS

4 eggs, room temperature

1 cup (250ml, 8fl oz) coconut milk

¼ cup (15g, ½ oz) semi-sun-dried tomatoes, pureed

½ cup (50g, 2oz) coconut flour

½ tsp GF bicarbonate of soda

1½ tbsps dried rosemary leaves, finely chopped

½ tsp ground oregano

Pinch of salt

1-2 tbsps fresh rosemary

10 cherry tomatoes

2 tbsps olive oil

METHOD

1. Preheat the oven to 180°C (350°F, Gas Mark 4) and line a medium pizza tray with oiled baking paper.

2. Whisk together the eggs and the coconut milk. Stir in the tomato puree, flour, bicarb, chopped rosemary, oregano and salt.

3. Spread the mixture in an even layer on the tray.

4. Sprinkle the fresh rosemary over the batter and gently push the cherry tomatoes into the dough. Drizzle the olive oil over the top.

5. Bake for 20 minutes, until the bread is cooked through and browned.

6. Remove from oven and let cool for 10 minutes before cutting into desired shapes.

ZUCCHINI BREAD

INGREDIENTS

500g (1lb 2oz) zucchini, grated

2 large eggs, room temperature

½ cup (125ml, 4fl oz) milk

115g (4oz) butter

2 tbsps agave syrup

¾ cup (185ml, 6fl oz) olive oil

1½ cups (275g, 10oz) potato flour

¾ cup (95g, 3oz) brown rice flour

¾ cup (80g, 3oz) quinoa flour

2 tsps GF baking powder

¼ tsp GF bicarbonate of soda

¼ cup (40g, 1½ oz) raisins

¼ tsp nutmeg

1 tsp salt

½ cup (60g, 2oz) grated tasty cheese

METHOD

1. Preheat the oven to 180°C (350°F, Gas Mark 4) and line two 20 x 10cm (8 x 4in) loaf tins with greased baking paper.

2. Place the grated zucchini in a clean tea towel and twist the ends to squeeze out as much liquid from the zucchini as you can. Set aside.

3. In a separate mixing bowl, whisk together the eggs, milk, butter, agave and olive oil. Set aside.

4. Place the flours, baking powder, bicarb, raisins, nutmeg and salt in a large mixing bowl. Give a stir to mix everything through and make a well in the centre.

5. Tip the grated zucchini and the cheese into the flours and toss to coat them in flour.

6. Add the egg mixture and stir everything together until just combined.

7. Divide the mixture between the two loaf pans.

8. Bake for 50 minutes until golden brown on top or until a skewer inserted into the middle comes out clean.

9. Cool the loaves in the tins for 15 minutes then turn out onto a wire rack to cool. Serve warm.

PUMPKIN SCONES

INGREDIENTS

3 cups (375g, 12oz) GF plain flour

3 tsps GF baking powder

Pinch of salt

1 tsp xantham gum

Pinch of nutmeg

⅓ cup (50g, 2oz) light brown sugar

1 cup (225g, 8oz) pumpkin puree (see recipe page 17)

2 medium eggs, room temperature

50g (2oz) unsalted butter, melted

¼ cup (60ml, 2fl oz) milk

½ cup (65g, 2oz) pepitas (pumpkin seeds)

METHOD

1. Preheat the oven to 200°C (400°F, Gas Mark 6) and line a large baking tray with baking paper.

2. Sift together the flour, baking powder, salt, xanthan gum, nutmeg and sugar into a large mixing bowl and give a stir to mix everything through then make a well in the centre.

3. Stir together the pumpkin puree, eggs and butter and pour into the flour mix. Fold the mixture until it forms a dough.

4. Tip the dough out onto a lightly floured work surface and knead gently. Push the dough out into a round about 3cm (1in) thick.

5. Use a sharp scone cutter to cut the dough into rounds, reusing the leftover dough to make more.

6. Place them about 1cm (½ in) apart on the tray and brush with milk then gently sprinkle the pepitas over the top.

7. Bake for 20 minutes or until golden and a skewer inserted into the centre comes out clean. Let cool on a wire rack for 10 minutes, then serve warm.

CORNBREAD MUFFINS

INGREDIENTS

160g (6oz) unsalted butter, room temperature

¾ cup (165g, 6oz) caster sugar

3 eggs, room temperature

¾ cup (120g, 4oz) fine polenta

2 tsps GF baking powder

1½ cups (180g, 6oz) almond meal

¼ tsp vanilla extract

METHOD

1. Preheat the oven to 180°C (350°F, Gas Mark 4) and line a 12-hole muffin tin with muffin liners.

2. Beat together the butter and sugar until they resemble whipped cream.

3. Stir in the eggs, one at a time, ensuring each is fully incorporated before adding the next.

4. Add the polenta in thirds, stirring until just combined each time before adding the next portion.

5. Stir in the baking powder, almond meal and vanilla until combined.

6. Spoon the mix into the 12 muffin liners.

7. Bake for 25 minutes until golden on top or a skewer inserted into the middle comes out clean.

8. Remove the muffins to a wire rack to cool for 20 minutes before eating.

SERVES 6-8 ★ PREP 20MIN ★ COOK TIME 1HR 5MIN

MEATLOAF

INGREDIENTS

2 tbsps unsalted butter

1 large onion, chopped

700g (1½ lb) minced beef

300g (10oz) minced veal

200g (7oz) bacon, roughly chopped

⅓ cup (80ml, 3fl oz) creme fraiche

½ cup (60g, 2oz) GF breadcrumbs

1 tbsp tomato paste

2 tsps ground oregano

¼ tsp nutmeg

Salt and pepper

2 large eggs, lightly beaten

1 tbsp GF Worcestershire sauce

4 slices prosciutto, chopped

2 tbsps GF barbecue sauce

½ tsp rosemary leaves, chopped

METHOD

1. Preheat the oven to 190°C (375°F, Gas Mark 5) and line a large loaf tin with oiled baking paper.

2. Melt the butter in a large saucepan over medium-high heat. Add the onion and fry for 5 minutes until softened and browned. Set aside.

3. Place the minced beef, veal, bacon, creme fraiche, breadcrumbs, tomato paste, oregano, nutmeg and a couple of good grinds of salt and pepper in a large mixing bowl. Add the cooked onions and use your hands to combine everything thoroughly.

4. Whisk the eggs and Worcestershire sauce together and add to the meat mixture. Mix through thoroughly.

5. Form the mix into a loaf shape and press into the tin, making the top slightly rounded.

6. Bake in the oven for 30 minutes then remove from the oven. Drain off any excess fat. Return to the oven for 20 minutes.

7. Stir together the prosciutto, barbecue sauce and rosemary and brush over the top of the meatloaf.

8. Return the loaf to the oven and bake for a further 15 minutes until browned on top.

9. Let the loaf cool for 15 minutes before serving.

KID-FRIENDLY

BLACK BEAN CHOCOLATE CAKE

INGREDIENTS

1 x 400g (14oz) can black beans, rinsed and drained

½ cup (50g, 2oz) pomegranate seeds

5 large eggs, room temperature

1 tbsp vanilla extract

¾ cup (165g, 6oz) caster sugar

½ tsp salt

6 tbsps butter, room temperature, cubed

5 tbsps cocoa powder

1 tsp GF baking powder

½ tsp GF bicarbonate of soda

1¼ cups (200g, 7oz) GF milk chocolate chips

METHOD

1. Preheat the oven to 180°C (350°F, Gas Mark 4) and line 20 x 10cm (8 x 4in) loaf tin with greased baking paper.

2. Place the beans, pomegranate seeds, eggs, vanilla, sugar and salt into a food processor. Process until the beans and pomegranate seeds have been broken down completely. Add the remaining ingredients, except for the chocolate chips, and process until everything is mixed through.

3. Remove the cake mix to a large mixing bowl and stir through the chocolate chips.

4. Pour the cake mix into the tin and smooth the top with a spatula.

5. Bake for 30 minutes until browned or until a skewer inserted into the middle comes out clean.

6. Let cool for 10 minutes in the tin before turning out onto a wire rack to cool.

ZUCCHINI BITES

INGREDIENTS

2 tbsps olive oil

3 cups (675g, 1½ lb) grated zucchini

9 eggs, room temperature

¼ cup (60ml, 2fl oz) milk

Salt and pepper

⅔ cup (115g, 4oz) corn kernels

½ cup (50g, 2oz) Parmesan cheese, grated

1 tbsp dried mixed herbs

½ cup (50g, 2oz) coconut flour

METHOD

1. Preheat the oven to 200°C (400°F, Gas Mark 6) and grease 24 small cupcake holes with olive oil.

2. Place the grated zucchini in a clean tea towel and twist the ends to squeeze out as much liquid from the zucchini as you can. Set aside.

3. Lightly beat the eggs in a large mixing bowl and then whisk in the milk and a couple of good grinds of salt and pepper.

4. Add the zucchini, corn, cheese and herbs and stir to combine. Sprinkle the coconut flour over the top and stir through until fully incorporated.

5. Pour the mixture into the 24 cupcake holes, filling them three-quarters full.

6. Bake for 20 minutes or until browned on top.

7. Let them cool for 10 minutes before serving.

CHICKEN MINI MEATBALLS

INGREDIENTS

Coconut oil, for frying

¼ cup (5g, ¼ oz) coriander leaves, to garnish

Lime wedges, to serve

Meatballs

500g (1lb 2oz) chicken thigh fillets, fat trimmed, roughly chopped

¼ cup (10g, ¼ oz) parsley leaves, finely chopped

3 tbsps GF breadcrumbs

2 garlic cloves, crushed

¼ cup (25g, 1oz) Parmesan, finely grated

2 tsps ground oregano

2 tsps lime zest

1 tbsp lime juice

2 tsps GF Worcestershire sauce

½ tsp salt

METHOD

1. Place all the meatball ingredients in the bowl of a food processor, pulse a few times and then process until the chicken is minced and all ingredients are thoroughly incorporated.

2. Using wet hands, roll spoonfuls of the mixture into small, walnut-sized balls.

3. Cover with plastic wrap and chill in the refrigerator for at least 1 hour before cooking.

4. Heat a large frying pan over medium-high heat. Melt 1 tablespoon of coconut oil and fry the meatballs in small batches for 8 minutes, until browned all over, turning constantly to cook on all sides. (If you overcrowd the meatballs, they won't brown, they'll poach instead.)

5. Let them cool for 5 minutes before serving.

6. Garnish with coriander leaves and lime wedges.

INARI SUSHI TEDDIES

INGREDIENTS

1½ tbsps white sesame seeds

1½ cups (235g, 7oz) uncooked sushi rice

2 cups (500ml, 1pt) cold water

¼ cup (50ml, 2fl oz) white wine vinegar

¼ cup (50ml, 2fl oz) rice wine vinegar

¼ cup (50g, 2oz) caster sugar

1½ tbsps salt

1 pack of 12 aburage (tofu pouches)

1 tsp butter

1 egg, lightly beaten

4 mini bocconcini, drained

2 seaweed sheets

METHOD

1. First, toast the sesame seeds. Preheat a small frying pan over medium-high heat. Dry fry the seeds for about 4 minutes or until they start to brown. Remove them immediately from the pan and set aside.

2. To make the rice, rinse it five times, then drain and let it dry for 20 minutes.

3. Place the rice and cold water in a medium saucepan and bring to a boil. Reduce heat to a simmer and cook, covered, for 20 minutes or until tender. Remove from the heat and let stand, covered, for 15 minutes.

4. Combine the white wine vinegar, rice wine vinegar, sugar and salt together in a small saucepan and heat over medium-high heat. Stir until the sugar is dissolved.

5. Sprinkle evenly over the rice and stir to mix through. Spread the rice out over a tray and fan to cool it down before using.

6. Boil the pouches in their packaging for 5 minutes. Drain and let them cool for 15 minutes.

7. Place a couple of spoonfuls of rice in one pouch and tuck the ends over each other and sit, seam side down. Repeat with the rest of the pouches and the rice.

8. Heat the butter in a small non-stick frying pan over medium-low heat. Beat the egg and pour into the pan in a thin layer. Cook for 1 minute on each side or until cooked through. Carefully lift out of the pan onto a plate and let cool.

9. To make the teddy faces, cut the bocconcini into thin circles for the muzzle. Cut the egg into little rounded triangles for the ears. Cut the seaweed into small circles for the eyes and nose and short strips for the mouth. Use a little water on the tip of your finger to stick the decorations onto the sushi pouches.

VEGGIE CHIPS

INGREDIENTS

3 medium beetroots, peeled

1 large thin sweet potato, peeled (choose a similar size as the beetroot chips)

2 tbsps olive oil

2 tbsps salt

METHOD

1. Preheat the oven to 180°C (350°F, Gas Mark 4) and line two large flat baking trays with baking paper.

2. Use a mandolin to slice the beetroot and sweet potato into 1 or 2mm (⅛ in) thick slices (the thinner they are, the crispier they'll be).

3. Toss the chips in a large bowl with the oil until they're well coated. Add more oil if needed.

4. Spread out in a single layer on the trays and sprinkle with salt. Bake for 15 minutes, then turn them over and bake for another 10 minutes until they're crispy. Keep an eye on them so they don't burn.

5. Let them cool in the oven on the tray with the door open. Serve.

CHEESY POTATO SPIRALS

INGREDIENTS

1²/₃ cups (375g, 13oz) Desiree potatoes, peeled and cubed

1 large egg, lightly beaten

2 tbsps arrowroot flour

2 tbsps Romano cheese

Salt and pepper

3 tbsps milk

Canola oil, for frying

1 tbsp sweet paprika (optional)

METHOD

1. Steam the potatoes for 15 minutes until soft.

2. Place in a large mixing bowl and mash until smooth.

3. Whisk in the egg, arrowroot flour, Romano, a couple of good grinds of salt and pepper and the milk and combine thoroughly.

4. Transfer into a piping bag with a 5mm (¼ in) round nozzle.

5. Heat enough oil to come at least 2cm (1in) up the sides of a medium deep-sided frying pan over medium-high heat.

6. Pipe spirals of the potato mixture, working from the inside out, into the oil.

7. Fry the spirals until brown and crispy. Drain on paper towels and sprinkle with paprika.

8. Serve warm with tomato sauce on the side.

RASPBERRY FUDGE BROWNIES

INGREDIENTS

150g (5oz) GF dark cooking chocolate, roughly chopped

100g (3½ oz) butter, room temperature, cubed

1 tsp vanilla extract

1 cup (135g, 5oz) light brown sugar

2 large eggs, room temperature

¼ cup (60ml, 2fl oz) coconut milk

¼ cup (30g, 1oz) raw cacao powder, plus 1 tbsp for dusting

2 tbsps coconut flour

¾ tsp GF baking powder

½ cup (50g, 2oz) almond meal

1¼ cups (155g, 5oz) frozen raspberries

Handful fresh raspberries, to garnish

METHOD

1. Preheat the oven to 160°C (325°F, Gas Mark 3) and grease and line a 16 x 26cm (6 x 10in) slice tin with greased baking paper.

2. Melt the chocolate and butter in a large heatproof bowl over a saucepan of simmering water. Remove from the heat and let cool for 10 minutes, then gently stir in the vanilla.

3. Add the sugar, eggs and coconut milk and stir until everything is thoroughly incorporated.

4. Sift the cacao powder, flour and baking powder together in a separate bowl and add the almond meal. Mix through then gradually stir into the wet ingredients until everything is barely mixed through.

5. Add the frozen raspberries and stir through. Again, mix until everything is just combined.

6. Pour the batter into the tin and smooth it over evenly.

7. Bake for 35 minutes. Insert a skewer into the middle. If it comes out mostly clean, then you're done. You want these to be cooked but still be gooey and fudgy.

8. Let cool for 30 minutes before removing from the tin.

9. Dust with extra cacao powder and top with fresh raspberries.

10. Cut into squares and serve them warm and gooey.

HAM ROLLS

INGREDIENTS

4 eggs, room temperature

¼ cup (30g, 1oz) tasty cheese

¼ cup (60ml, 2fl oz) cream

Pinch of salt

2 tsps butter

8 slices honey leg ham

4 cherry tomatoes, halved

8 toothpicks

4 chives, chopped

METHOD

1. Whisk together the eggs, cheese, cream and salt until light and fluffy.

2. Heat a medium non-stick frying pan over medium heat and melt the butter.

3. Pour the egg mixture into the pan and let it cook for 30 seconds. Gently and slowly push the edges into the middle of the pan for 2 minutes or until the eggs are cooked through. Remove the eggs to a bowl and fluff up with a fork. Let them cool for 20 minutes.

4. Place ¼ cup of the eggs along the middle of each slice of ham. Place a cherry half, cut side down over the folded ends of the ham and secure the ham with a toothpick.

5. Repeat with the rest of the egg and the ham. Garnish with chives.

EGG ROLLS

INGREDIENTS

1 tbsp sesame oil

400g (14oz) firm tofu, cut into thin strips

1 tsp minced ginger

2 cups (200g, 7oz) cabbage, finely shredded

2 medium carrots, halved and julienned

200g (7oz) green beans, ends trimmed

3 spring onions, finely chopped

110g (4oz) bean sprouts, rinsed and drained

1 tbsp GF tamari sauce

12 egg roll wrappers

Canola or vegetable oil, for frying

METHOD

1. Heat the sesame oil in a medium non-stick frying pan over medium heat.

2. Gently heat the tofu and ginger for 2 minutes, then remove from the pan. Add the cabbage, carrots and beans and fry for another 2 minutes. Toss through the spring onions, sprouts and tamari and cook for 1 further minute. Remove the mixture to a bowl and let cool for 10 minutes.

3. Use 2 tablespoons of the filling for each roll. Place a wrapper in a diamond shape and spread the filling along the middle.

4. Fold the bottom corner over the filling, then fold over the side corners. Brush the top corner with water and roll up the wrap tightly to enclose the filling. Seal the roll with the top flap.

5. Heat enough oil to come at least 1cm (½ in) up the side of a deep-sided frying pan. Fry a few rolls at time, placing them seam-side down to start with.

6. Fry each roll for 3 minutes, turning occasionally. Drain on paper towels. Serve hot.

CHOCOLATE MINT PARFAIT

INGREDIENTS

3 cups crumbled black
bean chocolate cake
(see recipe page 190)

Custard

1 tsp vanilla extract

1½ cups (375ml, 13fl oz)
milk

1 cup (250ml, 8fl oz)
thickened cream

6 egg yolks, room
temperature

½ cup (110g, 4oz) caster
sugar

2 tsps arrowroot flour

Mint topping

150g (5oz) GF white
cooking chocolate,
roughly chopped

½ tsp peppermint
essence

2½ cups (600ml, 21fl oz)
thickened cream

Green food colouring

METHOD

1. To make the custard, place the vanilla and milk in a saucepan over low heat. Stir for 3 minutes, then add the cream. Increase heat to medium and use a whisk to stir until almost simmering.

2. Remove from the heat, cover with a tight-fitting lid and sit for 15 minutes.

3. Whisk together the egg yolks, sugar and arrowroot flour in a medium saucepan for 5 minutes until pale and creamy and at least doubled in size. Pour in ¼ cup of the warm milk mixture and whisk through.

4. Heat the saucepan over medium heat and gradually whisk in the rest of milk mixture. Stir for 12 minutes or until the custard is thick enough to coat the back of a spoon. Remove from the heat into a pouring jug, cover and let it cool in the refrigerator for at least 2 hours before using.

5. To make the mint topping, place the white chocolate, peppermint essence, and half the cream in a small saucepan over low heat. Gently stir until the chocolate is melted. Place the mix in the refrigerator and chill for at least 2 hours.

6. Beat the rest of the cream until soft peaks form. Fold in the white chocolate mixture. Then divide the mix in half and colour one half with a couple of drops of green food colouring.

7. To assemble, place a large spoonful of cake in the bottom of each of four mason jars. Top with a spoonful of green chocolate mixture then add a layer of 2 spoonfuls of custard. Top with more cake, then a couple of spoons of the white chocolate cream. Pour over some more green chocolate cream and then sprinkle over some more cake mixture. Serve.

BANANA CHIPS

SERVES 4 ★ PREP 15MIN ★ COOK TIME 15MIN

INGREDIENTS

4 almost yellow bananas, peeled and cut into 3mm (⅛ in) thick slices

3 cups (750ml, 24fl oz) water

2 cups (500ml, 1pt) coconut oil

Salt, to taste

METHOD

1. Place the slices in a bowl with the water for 5 minutes, then drain them in a colander.

2. Heat the oil in a deep-frying saucepan over high heat.

3. Test whether the oil is hot enough by dropping one slice in the saucepan. If it bubbles and rises to the top, the oil is hot enough.

4. Add the slices in small batches and fry for about 2 minutes or until they're golden.

5. Drain the chips on paper towels and sprinkle with salt to taste.

6. Serve warm or cold.

ALMOND BANANA MUFFINS

INGREDIENTS

2 medium ripe bananas

2 tbsps agave syrup

2 tbsps milk

1 tsp vanilla extract

½ tsp lemon juice

2 tbsps unsalted butter, melted

½ cup (110g, 4oz) caster sugar

⅓ cup (40g, 1½ oz) almond meal

⅔ cup (65g, 2oz) coconut flour

¼ cup (30g, 1oz) tapioca flour

½ tsp xanthan gum

1½ tsps GF baking powder

½ tsp GF bicarbonate of soda

Pinch of salt

¾ tsp allspice

⅓ cup (50g, 2oz) GF milk chocolate chips

METHOD

1. Preheat the oven to 200°C (400°F, Gas Mark 6) and line 12 muffin holes with muffin liners.

2. Mash the bananas in a large bowl then add the agave syrup, milk, vanilla, lemon juice, butter and caster sugar.

3. Stir until everything is thoroughly incorporated.

4. Add the rest of the ingredients except the chocolate chips to a separate bowl and stir to combine.

5. Whisk the dry ingredients into the banana mixture a third at a time, ensuring each portion is just mixed through before adding the next portion. Fold in the chocolate chips.

6. Drop the muffin batter into the liners to three-quarters full.

7. Bake for 25 minutes until browned or until a skewer inserted into the middle comes out clean.

8. Cool in the tin for 5 minutes before removing to a wire rack to cool completely.

SERVES 4 ★ PREP 1HR (PLUS CHILLING) ★ COOK TIME 40MIN

CHOCOLATE CARAMEL TARTS

INGREDIENTS

Tart shells

⅓ cup (40g, 1½ oz) macadamia nuts, chopped and toasted

1½ cups (185g, 6oz) GF plain flour

½ cup (80g, 3oz) dark brown sugar

¼ tsp salt

130g (4oz) unsalted butter, chilled and cubed

1 egg yolk, lightly beaten

Caramel

2 cups (440g, 1lb) caster sugar

½ cup (125ml, 4fl oz) water

⅓ cup (105g, 4oz) agave syrup

¾ tsp salt

½ cup (125ml, 4fl oz) thickened cream

115g (4oz) unsalted butter, room temperature

½ tsp vanilla paste

Chocolate

120g (4oz) GF unsweetened dark cooking chocolate, roughly chopped

⅓ cup (80ml, 3fl oz) thickened cream

2 tbsps unsalted butter, room temperature

Pinch of salt

½ tsp vanilla paste

2 tsps rock salt

METHOD

1. Preheat the oven to 190°C (375°F, Gas Mark 5).

2. To make shells, grease four small fluted tart cases. Place the macadamias in a food processor bowl and process to a fine meal. Add the flour, brown sugar and salt and pulse a couple more times. Scatter the butter over the mixture and pulse until the mixture resembles breadcrumbs. Add the egg and process until the mixture starts to come together to form a dough. Add a couple of teaspoons of chilled water if it's still too dry.

3. Remove the dough to a lightly floured workspace and knead for 1 minute. Mould it into a flattened disc, cover with plastic wrap and place in the refrigerator for 30 minutes.

4. Turn out onto a floured workspace again and divide into four pieces. Roll out each piece into a circle about 3mm (⅛ in) thick and press into the tart cases. Cover the pastry with foil, fill the cases with baking beads and bake for 15 minutes. Remove beads and foil and bake for another 5 minutes. Remove from oven and let them cool.

5. To make the caramel, heat sugar, water, agave and salt in a heavy saucepan over medium-high heat. Stir until the liquid begins to turn caramel, then remove from heat and whisk in the cream, butter and vanilla. It may start to foam but that's what it should do. Heat the mixture until it's barely simmering (115°C/243°F). Remove from heat and cool for 30 minutes then pour into the tart shells. Place in the refrigerator for ½ hour.

6. To make the chocolate layer, place the chocolate in a large mixing bowl. Heat the cream, butter and salt in a small saucepan over medium heat until nearly simmering. Pour the hot cream over the chocolate and add the vanilla. Let sit for 5 minutes to let the chocolate melt then use a whisk to gently mix everything together. Pour over the caramel layer and sprinkle some rock salt over the top.

7. Chill in the refrigerator until the chocolate is set.

LEMON BAR COOKIES

INGREDIENTS

Base

¼ tsp vanilla paste

⅓ cup (70g, 2½ oz) caster sugar

150g (5oz) unsalted butter, melted

1 tbsp arrowroot flour

1 cup (100g, 3½ oz) coconut flour

⅓ cup (50g, 2oz) rice flour

⅓ cup (30g, 1oz) desiccated coconut

Topping

4 large eggs, room temperature

2 tsps lemon zest

⅓ cup (40g, 1½ oz) tapioca flour

1⅓ cups (290g, 10oz) caster sugar, plus 2 tbsps for sprinkling

⅔ cup (160ml, 5fl oz) lemon juice

METHOD

1. Preheat the oven to 180°C (350°F, Gas Mark 4) and line a 16 x 26cm (6 x 10in) slice tin with greased baking paper, leaving 3cm (1in) of overhang.

2. Add the vanilla and sugar to the butter in a large mixing bowl and stir to combine. Sift the flours over the top and then mix through along with the coconut.

3. Press the mixture into the bottom of the slice tin in an even layer.

4. Bake for 20 minutes, then let cool to room temperature before moving to the next step.

5. To make the topping, whisk together the eggs, lemon zest, tapioca flour and sugar until the batter is smooth.

6. Pour in the lemon juice and mix through. Pour the lemon topping over the base.

7. Bake for 20 minutes. Remove from the oven and let it cool for 20 minutes in the tin before sprinkling with the extra sugar and placing it in the fridge to cool for at least 2 hours.

8. Once the topping has hardened, cut into desired shapes while still in the tin. Serve.

GINGERBREAD CUPCAKES

INGREDIENTS

Cupcakes

60g (2oz) extra firm silken tofu

½ cup (155g, 5oz) pure maple syrup

¾ cup (185ml, 6fl oz) milk

½ tsp vanilla paste

1 tsp apple cider vinegar

115g (4oz) unsalted butter, softened

½ cup (80g, 3oz) brown sugar

1⅓ cups (165g, 5½ oz) GF plain flour

1 tsp GF baking powder

½ tsp GF bicarbonate of soda

1 tsp ground ginger

1 tsp allspice

Pinch of nutmeg

Pinch of ground cloves

Pinch of salt

2 cups (450g, 1lb) buttercream frosting (see recipe page 220)

Butterscotch sauce

1 cup (250ml, 8fl oz) whipping cream

1 cup (155g, 5oz) light brown sugar

1 tbsp unsalted butter, chopped

2 tbsps golden syrup

½ tsp vanilla paste

METHOD

1. Preheat the oven to 180°C (350°F, Gas Mark 4) and line 12 cupcake holes with cupcake liners.

2. Place the tofu, pure maple syrup, ½ cup milk, vanilla and vinegar in a blender or use a stick blender to puree until smooth.

3. Beat the sugar and butter together until it resembles whipped cream. Beat in the tofu mix until combined. Sift in the dry ingredients and stir through then mix in the remaining milk.

4. Pour the batter into the cupcake liners to about three-quarters full. Bake for 25 minutes, or until a skewer inserted into the middle of a cupcake comes out clean. Cool on wire racks.

5. Spoon softened buttercream into a piping bag and pipe the icing onto the cooled cupcakes.

6. To make the butterscotch sauce, place all the sauce ingredients in a medium saucepan over medium-high heat. Stir until boiling, then reduce the heat and simmer for 8 minutes until the sauce is thickened and golden brown. Drizzle the sauce over the cupcakes. Serve.

SNICKERDOODLE COOKIES

INGREDIENTS

115g (4oz) unsalted butter, room temperature, cubed

60g (2oz) Copha

½ cup (110g, 4oz) caster sugar

¼ cup (40g, 1½ oz) light brown sugar

1 tsp vanilla paste

2 large eggs, room temperature

½ tsp GF bicarbonate of soda

¾ tsp salt

1 tsp cinnamon

Pinch of allspice

3 cups (300g, 10oz) almond flour (can use almond meal)

For the topping

¼ cup (55g, 2oz) caster sugar

2 tsps cinnamon

METHOD

1. Preheat the oven to 180°C (350°F, Gas Mark 4) and line a large baking tray with baking paper.

2. Place the butter, Copha and sugars in a stand mixer and mix until they resemble whipped cream. Add the vanilla and then the eggs one at a time, ensuring each egg is just mixed through before adding the next.

3. Mix together the bicarb, salt, cinnamon, allspice and flour in large bowl then add that to the egg mixture in thirds, ensuring each portion is thoroughly mixed through before adding the next.

4. Quickly mix the caster sugar and cinnamon for the topping together in a shallow dish.

5. Roll the dough into around 26 small balls and roll them in the cinnamon sugar to coat them.

6. Arrange them on the tray, about 5cm (2in) apart. Bake for 12 minutes, or until they begin to turn golden on the edges. Let them cool on the tray for 5 minutes, then remove them to a wire rack to cool.

PUMPKIN SCROLLS WITH CARAMEL SAUCE

INGREDIENTS

Rolls

½ cup (125ml, 4fl oz) milk

3 tbsps brown sugar

7g (¼ oz) dried yeast

1 large egg, room temperature, lightly beaten

¾ cup (170g, 6oz) pumpkin puree (see recipe page 17)

1 tbsp unsalted butter, melted

1½ cups (195g, 7oz) brown rice flour

½ cup (50g, 2oz) coconut flour

¼ cup (40g, 1½ oz) white rice flour

¼ cup (30g, 1oz) tapioca flour

1½ tsps baking powder

¾ cup (120g, 4oz) GF chocolate chips

1 tsp cinnamon

½ tsp allspice

Pinch of nutmeg

Pinch of ground cloves

Filling

3 tbsps unsalted butter, melted

⅓ cup (50g, 2oz) dark brown sugar

2 tbsps ground cinnamon

Caramel sauce (see recipe page 206), to serve

METHOD

1. To make the rolls, preheat the oven to 190°C (375°F, Gas Mark 5) and grease a large, shallow baking dish.

2. Warm the milk in a small saucepan. Pour into a large mixing bowl with the sugar and yeast and let it sit for 3 minutes. Whisk in the egg, pumpkin puree and butter and mix through.

3. Sift the flours into a separate bowl with the baking powder, chocolate chips and spices. Add the flours to the yeast mixture in thirds, ensuring each portion is just mixed through before adding the next, until it forms a dough.

4. Remove the dough to a lightly floured surface (use coconut flour) and knead for 2 minutes. Roll the dough out into a long rectangle. Brush the melted butter onto it and sprinkle over the dark brown sugar and cinnamon. Roll up from one of the longer ends to make a very long roll.

5. Cut it into 2cm (1in) thick slices. Arrange them loosely in the baking dish leaving about 2cm (1in) space between them. Brush some more melted butter over the top and cover with a tea towel. Place in a warm spot and let them rise for 30 minutes.

6. Bake for 20 minutes or until golden on top. Remove from the oven, warm up the caramel sauce and drizzle it over the scrolls. Serve warm.

PEANUTTY RICE PUFFS

INGREDIENTS

6 cups (95g, 3oz)
puffed rice cereal

½ cup (50g, 2oz)
desiccated coconut

40g (1½ oz) unsalted
butter

40g 1½ oz) GF cashew
butter

¼ cup (30g, 1oz) peanuts,
chopped

¼ cup (30g, 1oz) raw
cacao powder

3 tbsps pure maple syrup

Pinch of salt

METHOD

1. Line a large 20cm (8in) square slice tin with baking paper, leaving about 3cm (1in) overhang.

2. Mix the puffed rice and coconut together in a large bowl.

3. Place the butter, cashew butter, peanuts, cacao powder, maple syrup and salt in a medium saucepan over medium heat.

4. Stir until the butter is melted and the mixture is smooth.

5. Pour the peanut mixture into the puffed rice mix and stir to combine.

6. Pour the mixture into the slice tin and press down to smooth the top.

7. Chill in the refrigerator for at least 3 hours before cutting into desired shapes while still in the tin. Serve.

EASTER RICE KRISPIES

INGREDIENTS

4 tbsps Copha

280g (10oz) GF marshmallows

6 cups (90g, 3oz) puffed rice cereal

1 cup (155g, 5oz) pastel-coloured Smarties

METHOD

1. Line a large 20cm (8in) square slice tin with baking paper, leaving about 3cm (1in) overhang.

2. Heat the Copha in a large saucepan over medium heat. Add the marshmallows gradually and stir until melted.

3. Pour the marshmallow mixture over the puffed rice and stir through to combine everything thoroughly.

4. Press the mixture into the slice tin and smooth the top.

5. Press the Smarties into the slice. Place the tin in the refrigerator and chill for at least 2 hours to harden before cutting into desired shapes. Serve.

RASPBERRY ICE-CREAM POPS WITH CRUMBLE

INGREDIENTS

Ice cream

1½ cups (185g, 6oz) fresh or frozen raspberries

1 x 400ml (14fl oz) can coconut cream

3½ tbsps agave syrup

1 tsp vanilla extract

Crumble

¾ cup (100g, 3½ oz) almond meal

¼ cup (25g, ¾ oz) desiccated coconut

3 tbsps unsalted butter, room temperature

2 tbsps agave syrup

Pinch of salt

METHOD

1. To make the ice cream place the raspberries in a blender or use a stick blender to puree them until smooth.

2. Push the raspberries through a sieve to remove the seeds and any solids.

3. Place all the ice-cream ingredients in a large mixing bowl and stir until completely combined.

4. Pour the mix into an ice-cream machine and mix for 30 minutes.

5. Spoon the ice cream into four dessert moulds (around 140ml capacity) and stick small dessert spoons into the middle of the ice cream.

6. Freeze for at least 4 hours.

7. To make the crumble, preheat the oven to 150°C (300°F, Gas Mark 2) and line a baking tray with baking paper.

8. Place all the crumble ingredients in a food processor bowl and pulse until the mixture resembles crumbs.

9. Tip out on the baking tray in a thin even layer.

10. Bake for 10 minutes until golden. Let it cool to room temperature.

11. Just before serving, remove the ice-cream pops from the moulds and press the crumble into them. Serve.

GLAZED LEMON POPPYSEED MUFFINS

INGREDIENTS

Cupcakes

⅔ cup (90g, 3oz) brown rice flour

35g (1¼ oz) potato flour

20g (¾ oz) white rice flour

15g (½ oz) tapioca flour

2½ tbsps poppy seeds

1½ tsps GF baking powder

1 tsp GF bicarbonate of soda

¾ tsp xanthan gum

½ tsp salt

115g (4oz) unsalted butter, room temperature

⅔ cup (140g, 5oz) caster sugar

2 large eggs, room temperature

⅔ cup (160ml, 5fl oz) Greek yoghurt

2 tbsps lemon zest

2 tbsps lemon juice

Glaze

2 tbsps lemon juice

½ cup (80g, 3oz) pure icing sugar

METHOD

1. Preheat the oven to 180°C (350°F, Gas Mark 4) and line two 6-hole cupcake tins with cupcake liners.

2. Place flours, poppy seeds, baking powder, bicarb, xanthan gum and salt into a mixing bowl and stir to combine. Set aside.

3. In a separate mixing bowl, beat butter and sugar together until it resembles whipped cream. Add eggs one at a time, completely mixing each one in before adding the next. Beat in the yoghurt, lemon zest and lemon juice until smooth. Add the flour mix in thirds, ensuring each portion is just mixed through before adding the next. Spoon batter into the cupcake liners.

4. Bake for 25 minutes or until a skewer inserted in the centre comes out clean. Cool on a wire rack.

5. Meanwhile, add half the lemon juice to the icing sugar and stir through, add the rest in small amounts until the glaze is a thin liquid. Drizzle over the cupcakes and serve.

LEMON SHORTBREAD BISCUITS

INGREDIENTS

250g (9oz) unsalted butter, room temperature

1½ cups (240g, 7½ oz) fine polenta

¾ cup (120g, 4oz) rice flour

¾ cup (120g, 4oz) pure icing sugar

1 tsp finely grated lemon zest

METHOD

1. Preheat the oven to 150°C (300°F, Gas Mark 2) and line a large flat baking tray with baking paper.

2. Place all the shortbread ingredients into a food processor and pulse until you get a smooth dough.

3. Turn the dough out onto a lightly rice floured surface and roll out to about 1cm (½ in) thick.

4. Cut out into desired shortbread shapes and place them on the tray. Leave 2cm (1in) space between the biscuits.

5. Lightly prick with fork, then bake for 25 minutes until crisp.

6. Place on a wire rack to cool before serving.

HALLOWEEN CHOCOLATE CUPCAKES

INGREDIENTS

Cupcakes

2 cups (200g, 7oz) almond flour

2 tbsps coconut flour

¾ cup (90g, 3oz) raw cacao powder

¼ tsp salt

½ tsp GF baking powder

60g (2oz) unsalted butter

½ cup (110g, 4oz) caster sugar

4 large eggs, room temperature

½ cup (125ml, 4fl oz) milk

Buttercream frosting

225g (9oz) unsalted butter, room temperature

6 cups (930g, 2lb) pure icing sugar

2 tsps vanilla extract

¼ cup (60ml, 2fl oz) thickened cream

Decoration

Red, yellow, blue and green food colouring

Halloween themed cake toppings

METHOD

1. Preheat the oven to 180°C (350°F, Gas Mark 4) and line four 6-hole cupcakes holes with cupcake liners (you can reuse one tray and cook in batches).

2. Add the flours, cacao powder, salt and baking powder to a large mixing bowl and stir to mix through. Set aside.

3. In a separate large mixing bowl, beat the butter and sugar together until it resembles whipped cream. Add the eggs one at a time, completely mixing each one in before adding the next.

4. Add the flour mix and milk in alternating thirds, ensuring each portion is just mixed through before adding the next.

5. Spoon the cake mix into the cupcake liners, filling each about three-quarters full.

6. Bake for 25 minutes or until a skewer inserted into the middle of one of the cupcakes comes out clean. Let them cool for 5 minutes in the tin, then place them on a wire rack to cool.

7. To make the frosting, beat the butter and icing sugar together until the icing sugar is dissolved and the mixture is light and fluffy.

8. Stir together the vanilla and cream then gradually add to the butter mixture and whisk until the buttercream is soft and fluffy. Cover and set aside.

9. Divide the frosting into thirds, keep one portion as is, use the red and yellow colourings to make one portion orange, and use the blue and red to make the remaining portion purple.

10. Spoon the icing into separate piping bags and ice the cupcakes.

11. Top with candy corns, pipe a dot of melted chocolate onto white candy to make eyeballs, sprinkle with Halloween-themed candy.

INDEX

First Published in 2018 by Herron Book Distributors Pty Ltd
14 Manton St
Morningside
QLD 4170
www.herronbooks.com

Custom book production by Captain Honey Pty Ltd
12 Station St
Bangalow
NSW 2479
www.captainhoney.com.au

Cataloguing-in-Publication. A catalogue record for this book is available from the National Library of Australia

ISBN 978-0-947163-95-2

Images used under license from Shutterstock.com
Printed and bound in China by 1010 Printing International Limited

5 4 3 2   19 20 21 22

NOTES FOR THE READER

Preparation, cooking times and serving sizes vary according to the skill, agility and appetite of the cook and should be used as a guide only.

All reasonable efforts have been made to ensure the accuracy of the content in this book. Information in this book is not intended as a substitute for medical advice. The author and publisher cannot and do not accept any legal duty of care or responsibility in relation to the content in this book, and disclaim any liabilities relating to its use.